dinner secrets
gluten-free

dinner secrets
gluten-free

pamela moriarty

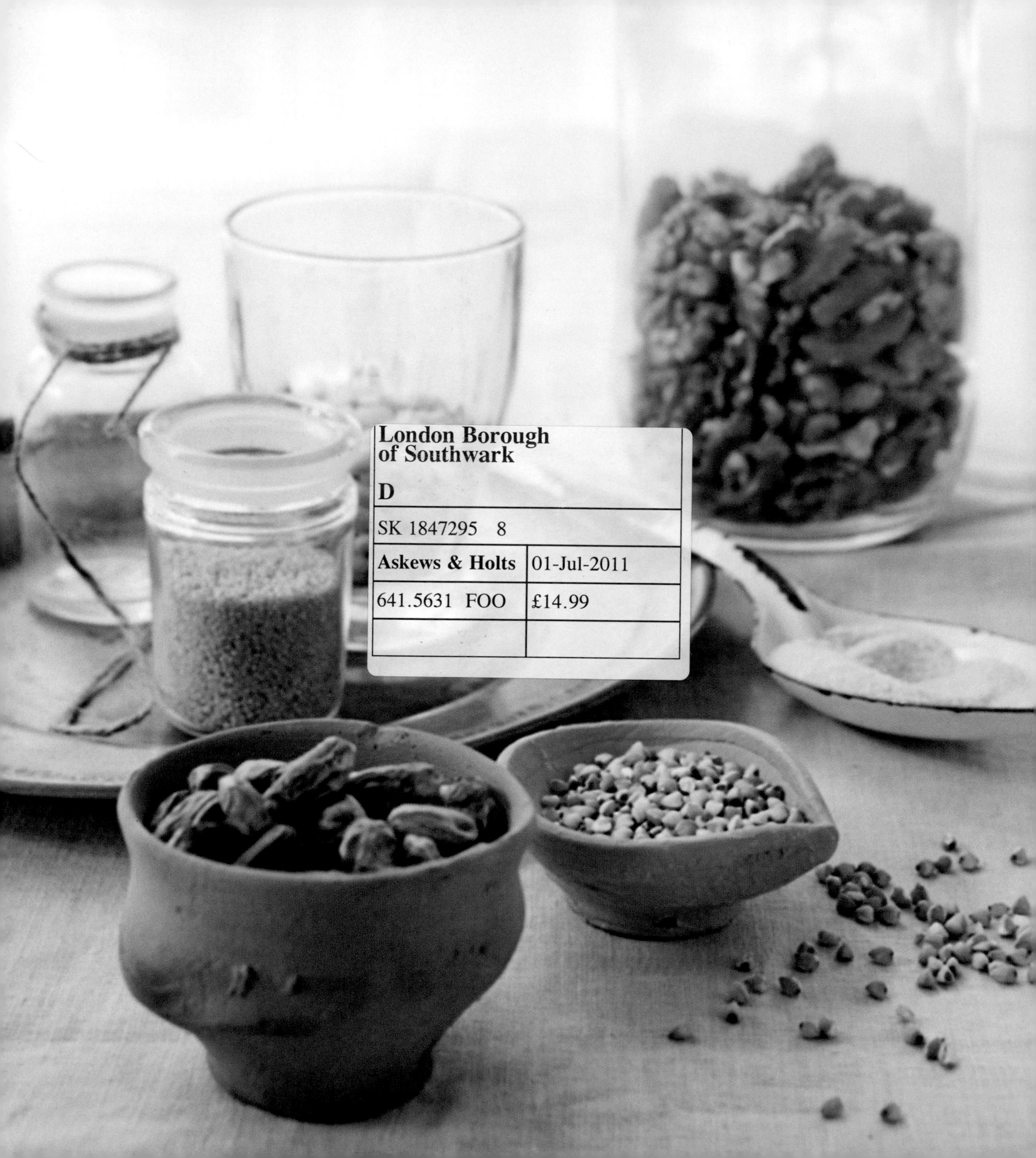

CONTENTS

INTRODUCTION

I cannot believe that I am writing the introduction to my second gluten-free cookbook. Many years after being diagnosed with coeliac disease, I ventured into writing *Sharing Sweet Secrets: Gluten & Wheat Free* because I craved desserts and sweet treats that tasted 'normal'. Having satisfied my sweet tooth, I decided to write *Dinner secrets*. This book is about cooking gluten-free food with a dash of panache. The Coeliac Society of Australia Inc has endorsed this cookbook, so you can rest assured that the ingredients used in the recipes are gluten free.

According to statistics, one in 100 people in Australia has coeliac disease but 75 per cent remain undiagnosed. That is, for every one person diagnosed there are probably three people unaware they have the condition. There are some others in the community who choose a wheat-free or gluten-free diet for perceived health benefits.

I was diagnosed with coeliac disease over 23 years ago. The diagnosis took about 18 months and by that time I was malnourished and anaemic, weighing just 35 kilograms (approximately 5½ stone). I was extremely ill, but within two weeks of eating gluten-free food, my health began to improve. I'd forgotten how wonderful it was to be well. I embraced the gluten-free diet because I felt so lucky to be able to manage coeliac disease by diet and not medication. I began to think about what food I could eat and enjoy, not about what I might be missing out on. It was not long before I realised that a gluten-free diet was the key to good health and well-being for people with coeliac disease or non-coeliac gluten intolerance.

Cooking, eating, reading about food, 'talking' food and creating recipes is what I do. This book contains mostly savoury food recipes with a small section on sweet food. They are recipes that I cook for family and friends and range from everyday quick and easy to entertaining with style. No one will ever realise that some ingredients are slightly different, as the end result is not only appealing to the eye, but full of flavour as well. Cooking gluten-free food is no more challenging than 'normal' cooking. You will be able to relax and enjoy yourself knowing that the food you have prepared will be safe and delicious for everyone.

Many of my recipes can be prepared in advance and finished with a minimum of fuss. There are chapters on party food, soup & light courses, mains, side dishes, sweet food and sauces & basics. I have included serving suggestions for the mains. You will also find savoury or sweet secrets that I share with you. These may include how to vary the recipe, substitute ingredients, information about a particular ingredient or an additional recipe suggestion. I hope you will find my cook's tips interesting and helpful too.

I'm amazed (and pleased) at how much things have changed since I was first diagnosed with coeliac disease. There were so few gluten-free products available and most were inedible. Food manufacturers have finally realised that there is a boom going on in gluten-free food. We are now spoilt for choice as most supermarkets and health food stores are stocking a large range of gluten-free flours including arrowroot, amaranth, brown and white rice, besan (chickpea flour), buckwheat, chestnut, soy, potato, tapioca, pure maize and quinoa. Manufactured gluten-free plain and self-raising flours are also readily available.

Coeliacs enjoy one of the healthiest diets around with emphasis placed on eating fresh, natural food. Many of my recipes are naturally gluten free but where you see **GF** next to manufactured products in the listed ingredients, it means to look for the gluten free equivalent. Foods that are naturally free from gluten include fish, meat, poultry, fats and oils, legumes, rice, millet, quinoa, fresh fruit and vegetables, herbs, nuts, eggs, milk and natural yoghurt (note: flavoured milk and flavoured yoghurt may contain gluten). Noodles and pasta made from rice, corn and buckwheat as well as polenta, which is one of my favourites, are all gluten free. Tea, coffee, most spirits and wine are also gluten free. We can even buy gluten-free beer now! One of my recipes for a light and crispy batter contains one of these gluten-free beers. What a treat for those of us with coeliac disease who cannot eat commercial fish and chips!

Where to begin? I find it helps to have a pantry well stocked with gluten-free ingredients. Having the basics on hand makes gluten-free cooking easy. My 'must haves' include gluten-free flours, pasta, noodles, rice, millet, quinoa, legumes, tins of tomatoes, gluten-free tomato paste (concentrated puree), fish sauce, soy sauce, tamari, worcestershire sauce, vinegars, chutneys and mustards. I like to have different types of oils including olive, vegetable, canola, grape seed, bran and sesame. I keep a good supply of nuts and dried fruit in my pantry too. Essentials in my refrigerator are butter, free-range eggs, milk, cream, ricotta, yoghurt and cheese. I always look for quality and flavour when purchasing seasonal fruit and vegetables.

One of our staples of course, is gluten-free bread. I've often heard people complain about the taste of it but I think the quality has improved so much over the years, and where would we be without it? I keep loaves frozen and always have gluten-free breadcrumbs in the freezer. I use them in stuffing mixtures, sweet and savoury crumbles and in tortes. I like to make my own stocks too because they are far superior in flavour and nutrition to any commercial stock cubes or boosters. I freeze stock in portions ready to use in soup, sauces and risotto. Like most people, I do occasionally resort to gluten-free stock cubes for convenience (as you will see in my recipes) but generally speaking, nothing beats a good home-made stock. The listed ingredients in all of my recipes are readily available in supermarkets, health food and speciality stores.

I hope you will find the ideas and easy-to-follow recipes in *Dinner Secrets: Gluten-free* imaginative and inspirational. You will be able to cook delicious food with that dash of panache suitable for any occasion, whether for a cocktail party, brunch, lunch or dinner.

Happy cooking and dining!

Endorsed by the Coeliac Society of Australia.

RECIPE AND INGREDIENT INFORMATION

Measurements

I have used the Australian 20 ml tablespoon measure, which is equal to 4 teaspoons. If you are using a 15 ml tablespoon, equal to 3 teaspoons, for most recipes the difference will not be noticeable. However, if using baking powder, bicarbonate of soda (baking soda) or gelatine, add an extra teaspoon for each tablespoon used.

All spoon and cup measurements are level unless stated to the contrary in a recipe.

Oven temperatures

For fan-forced ovens, as a general rule you will need to set the oven temperature 20°C (35°F) lower than indicated in the recipe.

Ingredients

When choosing ingredients, always read the labels carefully as companies do change their product ingredients from time to time. The gluten-free logo (crossed grain logo) consists of an ear of wheat with a line struck through the centre and is often used on packaging. The crossed grain logo is a trademark owned and controlled by the Coeliac Society of Australia Inc under a licence agreement. Companies who use this logo have to meet strict criteria, where their products are regularly analysed to ensure they maintain consistency in their gluten-free status.

In Australia, all foods must comply with the Food Standards of Australia and New Zealand Code for food labelling. The purpose of a strict labelling code is to allow consumers to make an informed choice. As a result the claim 'gluten-free' is specifically defined. Also, under the code, if an ingredient is derived from wheat, rye, barley or oats, then it must be declared on all packaging. However, keep in mind that there are many products that are naturally gluten free, but it is always wise to check ingredients listed on labels.

Where you see **GF** (meaning gluten-free) in bold capital letters next to certain manufactured products in the listed ingredients, it means to look for the gluten-free equivalent in the supermarket, health food or speciality store.

Those who might be at risk from the effects of salmonella poisoning (the elderly, pregnant women, young children and anyone with immune-deficiency diseases) should consult their doctor with any concerns about eating raw eggs, as for example, in my whole-egg mayonnaise recipe.

I mostly use fresh herbs when cooking so unless I have specified 'dried', fresh is best. The same goes for citrus juices (lemon, lime, orange, etc.). Where juice is used in a recipe, I always use freshly squeezed.

UNDERSTANDING COELIAC DISEASE — A BRIEF EXPLANATION

Coeliac disease (pronounced seel-ee-ack) is an autoimmune disease. This means the body mistakenly produces antibodies that damage its own tissues. Coeliac disease is a permanent intestinal intolerance to dietary gluten found in barley, wheat, oats and rye. A number of serious health consequences can result if the condition is not diagnosed and treated properly. In those with untreated coeliac disease, the mucosa (lining) of the small bowel (small intestine) is damaged: the tiny, finger-like projections that line the bowel (villi) become flattened and inflamed. The function of this mucosa is to break down and absorb nutrients in food.

Symptoms

The symptoms of coeliac disease reflect the consequences of chronic malabsorption and may include the following:
* severe diarrhoea, rumbling stomach, flatulence, stomach distension, constipation, bloating and cramping
* nausea and vomiting
* fatigue, weakness, lethargy, tiredness and irritability
* anaemia — an iron or folic acid deficiency is common
* recurrent mouth ulcers and/or swelling of mouth or tongue
* bone and joint pain
* weight loss — although many people do not lose weight and some can even gain weight.

Who gets coeliac disease and how is it diagnosed?

People are born with a genetic predisposition to developing coeliac disease. They inherit a particular genetic make up (HLA type) with the genes DQ2 and DQ8 being identified as the 'coeliac genes'. Gene testing is presently available through pathology laboratories (by blood test or oral swab). The gene test is useful for excluding coeliac disease. 'At risk' groups include first-degree relatives of a person with coeliac disease and those with type 1 diabetes or other autoimmune conditions. People belonging to these groups should be screened for coeliac disease.

Coeliac blood tests are used for initial screening ('coeliac serology and IgA'). If the results are positive, further testing is warranted. A gastroenterologist will perform a gastroscopy (an endoscope is passed through the mouth into the small bowel) to collect tiny samples (biopsies) from the small bowel. The biopsy is examined under a microscope to determine if coeliac disease is present. A second biopsy is usually performed after 12 months on a gluten-free diet to show that bowel repair has occurred.

Treatment

Strict adherence to a gluten-free diet for life is the only treatment for coeliac disease.

Note

This is not a medical book. The above information should be used as a guide only. If you are unwell and suspect coeliac disease, seek professional advice from a qualified medical practitioner and Accredited Practising Dietitian (APD). A good source for finding an APD in your local area is by visiting the Dietitians Association of Australia (DAA) website: www.daa.asn.au.

Resources

The Coeliac Society of Australia Inc has a number of useful and practical resources. Each state has its own office from which you can obtain information and support on coeliac disease and the gluten-free diet. They are also able to put you in touch with local groups and inform you about upcoming events that are of interest to people with coeliac disease. Coeliac societies also increase awareness within the food industry and fund research into the coeliac condition. A comprehensive guide to gluten-free ingredients is available with membership through your state Coeliac Society. The Society website is www.coeliacsociety.com.au.

PARTY FOODS

chickpea flat bread

Besan is roasted chickpea flour with a creamy colour. Nutritious and tasty, I cannot resist eating the first flat bread straight out of the pan! These flat breads are very satisfying and can be eaten a number of ways. See savoury secrets for variations.

MAKES 5 FLAT BREADS

110 g (3¾ oz/1 cup) besan (chickpea flour)

2½ tablespoons olive oil

zest of 1 lemon, finely grated

2 teaspoons sumac* (optional)

bran oil, for frying

place besan in a food processor. Combine 250 ml (9 fl oz/1 cup) water and olive oil in a small jug. With the motor running, slowly pour the mixture through the feed tube. Scrape down the sides of the bowl.

add zest, sumac, if using, and salt, to taste. Process again. Transfer batter to a jug so that it is easy to pour.

heat a 24 cm (9½ inch) non-stick crepe pan over medium–high heat. Add 1 teaspoon of bran oil and pour in one-fifth of the batter. Tilt and swirl pan so batter covers the base.

cook until bread sets on top and browns lightly on the bottom. This will take about 1 minute. Turn to cook other side. Slide flat bread onto a wire rack.

stir batter between making each flat bread. Thin batter with a little water if necessary. Add 1 teaspoon of bran oil to the pan before making each flat bread. Continue until you have used all of the batter.

SAVOURY SECRETS

Sumac* is a lemony spice available from some supermarkets and Middle Eastern grocery stores.

This is a very versatile recipe. Use the flat bread as you would a wrap or savoury crepe. Cut in wedges to serve with dips or tapenade and soft goat's curd.

To make **chunky chickpea & spring onion flat bread** prepare batter (as above), add 2 thinly sliced spring onions (scallions), 100 g (3½ oz/½ cup) drained and rinsed tinned chickpeas and 2 teaspoons ground cumin. Process batter briefly so that it retains some texture from the chickpeas. Thin chickpea batter with a little water if necessary. You can freeze remaining chickpeas from the tin or use them in another recipe.

To make **seeded chickpea flat bread** prepare batter (as above), add 2 teaspoons sesame seeds, and 1 teaspoon each poppy seeds and nigella seeds.

Chickpea flat bread may be frozen. Layer cooked flat bread with freezer wrap and place in a zip-lock bag or wrap in foil. For a soft texture, reheat flat bread in a microwave on high for 10 seconds or under the grill for crisp flat bread.

chorizo parsley puffs

Prepare the chorizo parsley mixture before you make the fail-proof choux pastry.

MAKES APPROXIMATELY 30

95 g (3¼ oz) **GF** chorizo sausage, thinly sliced

2 tablespoons roughly chopped flat-leaf (Italian) parsley

1 quantity **fail-proof choux pastry** (page 206)

line two baking trays with baking paper.

preheat oven to 200°C (400°F/Gas 6).

heat a small frying pan over medium heat. Add chorizo and cook until lightly browned (there is no need to add oil to the pan). Drain on paper towel.

place chorizo in a food processor and pulse to crumble. Combine with parsley, transfer to a bowl and set aside.

wipe processor bowl with paper towel.

prepare choux pastry.

add reserved chorizo and parsley mixture to the choux pastry and pulse to combine or fold in by hand.

place about 2 teaspoons of mixture, 5 cm (2 inches) apart on the prepared baking trays.

bake choux for 20–25 minutes until puffed and golden. Place on a wire rack to cool.

SAVOURY SECRETS
The puffs may be baked in advance and reheated in the oven until crisp to serve. They may also be frozen.

Substitute **GF** bacon for the **GF** chorizo.

To make **vegetarian puffs** replace **GF** chorizo with 2 tablespoons chopped semi-dried tomatoes, 1 or 2 tablespoons drained, rinsed and chopped capers, 1 tablespoon chopped pitted olives and 2 tablespoons chopped flat-leaf (Italian) parsley. Combine with choux pastry and bake as above.

dips

roasted beetroot dip

My daughter Kate contributed this recipe.
She suggests baking extra beetroot and using
the remainder in a salad or serving it as a warm
vegetable with crème fraîche.

MAKES ABOUT 250G (9 OZ/1 CUP)

3 beetroot (beets), rinsed well

2 teaspoons olive oil, plus extra, to brush

125 g (4½ oz/½ cup) **GF** Greek-style yoghurt

½ teaspoon garam masala

½ teaspoon ground cumin

½ teaspoon ground coriander

2 teaspoons lemon juice

½ teaspoon roasted cumin seeds, to finish

preheat oven to 180°C (350°F/Gas 4).

place beetroot on a sheet of foil, brush with extra olive oil
and wrap in the foil. Place on a baking tray and bake for
1 hour or until tender when pierced with a skewer. Cool
beetroot and, wearing latex gloves, peel.

chop beetroot roughly and place in a food processor.
Add 2 teaspoons olive oil, yoghurt, spices and lemon juice.
Season with salt and freshly ground black pepper and
process until smooth. Spoon dip into a bowl and sprinkle
with roasted cumin seeds.

serve with **chickpea flat breads** (page 14) or **GF** crackers.

SAVOURY SECRET
To make **quick yoghurt dip** add 1–2 teaspoons harissa paste to
250 g (9 oz/1 cup) **GF** Greek-style yoghurt. Add freshly
chopped coriander (cilantro) leaves, to finish.

spicy sweet potato dip

MAKES ABOUT 500G (1 LB 2 OZ/2 CUPS)

20 g (¾ oz) unsalted butter, melted

1 garlic clove, crushed

350 g (12 oz) sweet potato, peeled and cut into chunks
or rounds

½ teaspoon sweet smoked paprika, plus extra, to finish

1 teaspoon olive oil, plus extra, to drizzle

2 spring onions (scallions), finely chopped

20 g (¾ oz) grated fresh ginger

1 fresh red chilli, seeded and finely chopped, to taste

110 g (3¾ oz/½ cup) tinned butterbeans (lima beans),
drained and rinsed

1 lemon or lime, zest and juice

line a baking tray with baking paper.

preheat oven to 180°C (350°F/Gas 4).

combine butter and garlic, brush all over sweet potato
and sprinkle with paprika. Place on prepared baking tray
and bake for 25 minutes or until tender.

heat a small frying pan over medium heat. Add olive oil
and any remaining garlic butter to the pan. Add spring
onion, ginger and chilli and sauté until the mixture
has softened.

transfer sweet potato and the spring onion mixture to a
food processor. Whizz to purée, scrape down sides of the
processor. Add butterbeans, zest and juice and purée until
smooth. Transfer dip to a bowl, drizzle with olive oil and
sprinkle with paprika.

serve with **chickpea flat breads** (page 14) or **GF** crackers.

éclairs with smoked salmon & horseradish cream

These wonderful little éclairs never fail to please. They are the perfect finger food as they can be prepared several weeks in advance, frozen, then simply defrosted and filled several hours before your guests arrive.

MAKES APPROXIMATELY 24

éclairs

1 quantity **fail-proof choux pastry** (page 206)

horseradish cream

200 g (7 oz) cream cheese, cut into small cubes

2 tablespoons **GF** prepared horseradish

zest of 1 lemon, finely grated

1 tablespoon finely chopped flat-leaf (Italian) parsley or dill (optional)

additional ingredients

150 g (5½ oz) smoked salmon slices, cut into 5 x 2.5 cm (2 x 1 inch) pieces

line two baking trays with baking paper.

preheat oven to 200°C (400°F/Gas 6).

for the éclairs

fit piping (icing) bag with a 1.5 cm (⅝ inch) nozzle and pipe éclairs 5 cm (2 inches) in length onto prepared baking trays.

bake for 20–25 minutes until puffed, crisp and golden brown. Allow to cool on a wire rack.

for the horseradish cream

prepare horseradish cream using a food processor. With the motor running drop cream cheese cubes, one at a time, through the feed tube. Add horseradish, zest, herbs, if using, and season with freshly ground black pepper. Process well to combine.

fit piping bag with a 1 cm (½ inch) nozzle and fill with horseradish cream.

to finish éclairs

cut along the length of each éclair but not all the way through.

place a piece of salmon in the base of each éclair. The salmon should hang over the sides a little.

pipe horseradish cream along the length of salmon.

fold top of éclair over horseradish cream leaving a little cream exposed.

SAVOURY SECRETS
Fill éclairs or choux puffs with alternative fillings, for example rare roast beef with horseradish cream made as above, substituting crème fraîche for cream cheese. Soft goat's curd topped with caramelised onions is another option. If you choose either of these fillings, use a spoon instead of a piping bag to fill the éclairs or puffs.

grilled oysters with spinach & pine nuts

Oysters, you either love them or not. I'm a fan and often serve them with drinks. When serving, offer a small fork to your guests to dislodge the oyster from the shell. You can also serve the oysters as a starter.

MAKES 24

24 oysters on the half-shell, rinsed quickly if gritty, excess water removed

topping

35 g (1¼ oz/⅓ cup) day-old **GF** breadcrumbs*

50 g (1¾ oz) unsalted butter, softened

10 spinach leaves, blanched, drained on paper towel and finely chopped

2 tablespoons grated parmesan cheese

2 tablespoons chopped flat-leaf (Italian) parsley

1 tablespoon snipped chives

1 tablespoon pine nuts

zest of 1 lemon, finely grated

line a baking tray with rock salt or crumpled foil.

preheat grill (broiler) to high.

sit oysters on top of salt or foil on the baking tray. This will hold oysters steady.

place breadcrumbs in a bowl and use your fingers to rub in the butter. Add remaining ingredients and combine well.

spoon mixture on top of oysters.

grill for 2–3 minutes or until topping is golden.

serve immediately.

SAVOURY SECRETS

GF breadcrumbs* see **cook's tips— bread** (page 210).

Topping may be prepared several hours in advance. Cover and refrigerate until required. Spoon topping on top of oysters just before grilling.

To make **ashed brie & almond oysters** place very thin slices of ashed brie on top of oysters and scatter with almond slivers or pine nuts. Grill oysters for several minutes until brie melts and nuts turn golden brown. Ashed brie is available in the cheese or deli section of most supermarkets. For a special occasion, stand the grilled oysters in shot glasses to serve. Place a tiny piece of removable adhesive under the shot glasses to anchor them to a platter.

polenta pizza bites

You can make one large pizza instead of pizza bites. See savoury secret below.

MAKES APPROXIMATELY 40 PIECES

750 ml (26 fl oz/3 cups) **GF** chicken or **GF** vegetable stock (I use a **GF** stock cube for this recipe) or water instead of stock

90 g (3¼ oz) coarse polenta

90 g (3¼ oz) fine (one-minute) polenta

2 tablespoons chopped flat-leaf (Italian) parsley (optional)

2–3 tablespoons olive oil

1 garlic clove, crushed

GF tomato paste (concentrated purée) or other bottled **GF** tomato passata (puréed tomatoes) to spread on pizza bases

toppings

GF bacon or **GF** salami, red capsicums (peppers), pitted black olives, parmesan cheese and oregano.

Prosciutto, **GF** bacon or **GF** salami, preserved artichoke hearts, flat-leaf (Italian) parsley and grated parmesan cheese.

Roasted diced pumpkin (winter squash), crumbled feta, sliced pitted black olives and dusted with sweet paprika.

Mozzarella or bocconcini, semi-dried tomatoes or fresh cherry tomatoes, basil and a good grinding of black pepper.

Chargrilled and finely chopped vegetables including eggplant (aubergine), red capsicum (pepper), zucchini (courgette), topped with grated parmesan cheese and sprinkled with oregano.

line a 30 x 25 cm (12 x 10 inch) baking dish with baking paper, then line a baking tray with baking paper.

preheat oven to 180°C (350°F/Gas 4).

place stock or salt and water in a heavy-based saucepan over high heat and bring to the boil.

mix coarse and fine polenta together and pour into the boiling water in a thin, steady stream. Stir constantly with a wooden spoon.

reduce heat to a slow steady simmer and stir until polenta thickens. This takes about 3 minutes. When cooked a wooden spoon should stand upright in the polenta. Stir in parsley, if using.

spoon polenta into prepared baking dish and flatten with dampened hands or a spatula. To avoid burning your hands wear latex gloves. Cool polenta, cover with plastic wrap and refrigerate until firm.

turn polenta out of dish onto a flat surface and cut into small pieces measuring approximately 5 x 3 cm (2 x 1¼ inches).

combine oil and garlic and brush one side of each piece of polenta lightly with oil. Place oiled side down on prepared baking tray. Spread a little tomato paste on polenta pieces and add topping of your choice. Bake polenta pizza bites for about 15–20 minutes or until cheese is lightly browned.

SAVOURY SECRET

To prepare a large pizza on a baking paper lined pizza tray, brush the baking paper with garlic-flavoured oil before flattening polenta on the tray. Spread base with **GF** tomato paste or tomato passata and toppings of your choice. Bake as above.

seeded parmesan wafers

These crunchy crisp wafers are very easy to put together and are ever so more-ish. You can also try other seeds including mustard, cumin and caraway. Enjoy wafers with drinks or soup.

MAKES APPROXIMATELY 20

100 g (3½ oz/1 cup) finely grated parmesan cheese

2 teaspoons coarse polenta

2 teaspoons pure maize cornflour (cornstarch)

2 teaspoons white rice flour

1½ teaspoons nigella seeds*

1 teaspoon poppy seeds

1 teaspoon sesame seeds

2 teaspoons olive oil

1 x 60 g (2¼ oz) egg, white only

line two baking trays with baking paper.

preheat oven to 170°C (325°F/Gas 3).

place parmesan, polenta, cornflour, rice flour and seeds in a bowl. Stir to combine. Add olive oil and egg white and using your fingers bring the mixture together to make a dough.

place dough between two sheets of baking paper, flatten it a little, then using a rolling pin, roll the dough out thinly. Refrigerate for 15 minutes. Remove top sheet of baking paper and cut dough into irregular shapes with a knife or use pastry cutters to shape. Place wafers on prepared baking trays. Reshape if necessary.

bake for 10–12 minutes until golden, swapping baking trays halfway through cooking time. Leave to cool on trays for a few minutes before removing to a wire rack to cool completely.

store in an airtight container for 1 week.

SAVOURY SECRETS
Nigella seeds* are available from health food and speciality stores. They are jet black in colour, have an aromatic, smoky flavour and are popular in Middle Eastern and Indian cookery.

smoked salmon pinwheels

These pinwheels look very elegant and taste fabulous.

MAKES APPROXIMATELY 24

100 g (3½ oz) smoked salmon slices

cream cheese filling

100 g (3½ oz) cream cheese, cut into small cubes

20 g (¾ oz) preserved lemon*, pulp discarded, rind rinsed and finely chopped

2 teaspoons lemon juice

1 tablespoon chopped flat-leaf (Italian) parsley or snipped chives

additional ingredients

2 tablespoons capers, rinsed well if salted and drained on paper towel

2–3 Lebanese (short) cucumbers

place a sheet of freezer wrap measuring 40 x 15 cm (16 x 6 inches) on a flat surface. Form a rectangle with the salmon slices by placing them side by side (one up, one down) on the freezer wrap. Cut salmon to fill in gaps if necessary. You should now have a rectangle of salmon measuring approximately 30 x 9 cm (12 x 3½ inches).

prepare the cream cheese filling in a food processor. With the motor running, drop cubes of cream cheese, one at a time, through the feed tube. Add preserved lemon, lemon juice and parsley.

spread a thin coating of cream cheese filling over the salmon. Add a little extra lemon juice if cream cheese filling is too firm to spread. Sprinkle with capers.

roll the salmon into a long roll using the freezer wrap as a guide. Place in the refrigerator to firm. The roll can be prepared a day in advance.

peel cucumbers but leave some thin green strips. Score lengthways with a fork and cut into 5 mm (¼ inch) rounds. Place rounds on paper towel and cover with more paper towel to remove excess moisture.

cut roll into pinwheels approximately 1 cm (½ inch) thick using a very sharp thin-bladed knife. Place pinwheels on cucumber. Wipe blade between cuts.

SAVOURY SECRETS

Preserved lemon* is available in supermarkets or prepare **preserved lemons** (page 202).

Cucumber may be prepared several hours in advance. Leave it to rest on paper towel in refrigerator until required. Place salmon pinwheels on cucumber just before serving.

Substitute **GF** crackers for the cucumber rounds.

smoked salmon rosti rolls

The taste and texture of these rolls is sublime! You'll keep on coming back for more.

MAKES 20–24

potato rosti

300 g (10½ oz) all-purpose potatoes, such as desiree or sebago, peeled and coarsely grated

3 spring onions (scallions), finely chopped, or snipped chives

1 tablespoon baby capers, rinsed well if salted and drained on paper towel

additional ingredients

unsalted butter and bran oil for cooking the rosti

300 g (10½ oz) smoked salmon slices, cut into rectangles approximately 10 x 2 cm (4 x ¾ inches)

60 g (2¼ oz/¼ cup) **GF** prepared horseradish or **wasabi mayonnaise** (page 61)

line a bowl with several layers of paper towel. Place grated potato on top and cover with more paper towel. Press down firmly to remove excess moisture and leave to drain for several minutes.

discard paper towel and reserve grated potato in the bowl.

combine spring onion and capers with potato.

heat about 1 teaspoon each of butter and oil in a small non-stick frying pan.

place 5 or 6 small mounds about 2 teaspoons each of rosti mixture in the pan and fry over medium heat until golden and crisp on both sides. Drain on paper towel and set aside.

wipe frying pan with paper towel before making more rosti. Add another teaspoon each butter and oil. Cook rosti until you have used all the mixture.

spread each rectangle of salmon with prepared horseradish. Place a rosti on the salmon and roll up.

serving suggestion

To 'stand' the rosti rolls upright on a platter, place a salmon rosti roll upright on your work surface and push the base down gently but firmly. Place on platter and repeat with remaining rolls.

SAVOURY SECRETS

To vary the potato rosti add lemon zest and parsley to the mixture before frying.

To prepare potato rosti in advance, place the cooked rosti on a foil-lined baking tray. When you are ready to serve the rosti, pop them under the grill (broiler) to crisp. Be sure to watch the rosti as they will only take a minute to crisp. Cut smoked salmon into rectangles, place on a plate or tray, spread with prepared horseradish, cover and place in the refrigerator until you are ready to roll the rosti.

Prepare larger potato rosti to serve with grilled or pan-fried fish, chicken, beef or lamb.

Purée any pieces of leftover salmon with cream cheese, lemon juice and chives to make a spread or dip. Alternatively fold smoked salmon pieces through scrambled eggs to serve for breakfast.

stuffed black grapes

These grapes have to be one of my favourite finger foods as they not only taste superb, but can be prepared well in advance. They are perfect nibbles to have with a glass of Champagne.

MAKES 36

36 large black globe grapes

filling

75 g (2¾ oz) cream cheese, softened

75 g (2¾ oz) chèvre*, soft but firm, similar in texture to cream cheese

1 spring onion (scallion), white part only, very finely chopped

zest of 1 lime, finely grated, and reserve 1 teaspoon juice

additional ingredients

60 g (2¼ oz) toasted almonds, hazelnuts or walnuts, finely chopped

blend ingredients for the filling with some freshly ground black pepper in a food processor.

use a small sharp knife to cut the grapes in half lengthways to the centre, but do not cut all the way through. Remove seeds with a small teaspoon. Drain grapes on paper towel.

place a small teaspoon of the filling in each grape crevice, gently close grape leaving some of the cream cheese mixture exposed.

roll each filled grape, cream cheese side only, in nuts and place on a platter. Refrigerate until required.

SAVOURY SECRETS
Chèvre* is cheese made from goat's milk You can use cream cheese only if you wish but the chèvre adds a little something.

thai chicken patties on cucumber

These little morsels can be prepared well in advance and taste great cold. Larger patties can be prepared for a delicious main course.

MAKES APPROXIMATELY
20 PATTIES

thai chicken patties

250 g (9 oz) skinless, boneless chicken breast, roughly diced

2 spring onions (scallions), sliced

1 garlic clove, crushed

1 tablespoon chopped coriander (cilantro) leaves and stems

1 tablespoon chopped mint

3 teaspoons **GF** fish sauce

2 teaspoons grated fresh ginger

1 pinch of sugar

¼ teaspoon chilli paste or 1 red chilli, seeded and finely chopped, to taste

3 teaspoons potato flour

additional ingredients

peanut or bran oil for shallow-frying

2–3 Lebanese (short) cucumbers, peeled and cut into 5 mm (¼ inch) rounds

coriander (cilantro) leaves, to finish

GF sweet chilli sauce, to finish

place chicken in a food processor and whizz to mince. Remove from processor and set aside.

place remaining patty ingredients and some freshly ground black pepper in the processor and process to a paste. Add minced chicken and pulse to combine.

form mixture into even walnut-sized balls and then flatten to make small patties. Wet hands with water before forming the mixture into balls.

shallow pan-fry patties in oil. Drain on paper towel.

place patties on cucumber rounds and place a tiny amount of sweet chilli sauce on top. Garnish with a coriander leaf.

SAVOURY SECRETS
Substitute white-fleshed fish or pork fillet for the chicken.

To vary the recipe, add some drained and chopped water chestnuts to the patty mixture. You can also dip the patties in dried rice flakes before frying. Rice flakes are available from Asian grocery stores.

Prepare patties in advance. Freeze mixture raw. Defrost and cook on the day they are to be eaten.

Make larger patties for a main course. Serve with **GF** vermicelli noodles, shredded carrot, thinly sliced cucumber and chopped roasted peanuts. Serve in a butter leaf lettuce cup and top with a **GF** Asian dipping sauce or **GF** sweet chilli sauce.

white corn tortilla melts

Quesadillas is the correct name for these melts. I often make them for lunch as they are quick and delicious. If you are serving melts with drinks, omit the jalapeño, if you wish.

MAKES 12 QUARTERS OR 24 SMALLER
WEDGES TO HAVE WITH DRINKS

filling

125 g (4½ oz/1 cup) grated cheddar cheese

6 **GF** ham slices, diced

preserved sliced jalapeño peppers*,
to taste (optional)

2 or 3 small tomatoes, seeded and diced or
semi-dried tomatoes, chopped

chopped herbs, use whatever you have
available, such as parsley, coriander
(cilantro) or basil

additional ingredients

6 white corn tortillas**

bran oil, for shallow-frying

combine filling ingredients in a bowl.

brush one side of a tortilla generously with oil and place oiled side down on a flat surface. Spread one-third of the filling over the tortilla. Place another tortilla on top, brush with oil and set aside. Repeat with remaining tortillas. You should have three double-sided tortillas to fry.

heat a non-stick frying pan over medium–high heat. Carefully lift a prepared tortilla into the pan and fry for several minutes until golden brown. Slide tortilla onto a plate, cover with frying pan and invert back into the pan to cook the other side. Repeat with remaining tortillas.

serve cut into wedges.

serving suggestion
They are great served with **guacamole salsa** (page 146).

SAVOURY SECRETS
Preserved sliced jalapeño peppers* and white corn tortillas** are available in some supermarkets or health food stores.

Vary the fillings, anything that you put on a pizza you can put in tortillas. You need to add cheese so that the tortillas hold together when fried.

For a strong cheesy taste, mix grated parmesan with cheddar.

SOUPS AND LIGHT COURSES

asian rice congee

Rice congee or 'jook' is a classic Chinese breakfast dish that I love to eat for lunch and dinner too. It's a great pick-me-up if you're feeling the need for comfort food. There are no rules about what accompaniments can be add to the congee so use my suggestions as a guide only.

SERVES 8

220 g (7¾ oz/1 cup) white short-grain rice, rinsed well and drained

2.5 litres (87 fl oz/10 cups) hot water or **GF** chicken stock (**GF** stock cubes are fine for this recipe)

1 teaspoon salt

40 g (1½ oz) fresh ginger, peeled and grated

3 garlic cloves, crushed

5 makrut (kaffir lime) leaves

2 lemongrass stems, bruised (optional)

1 fresh red chilli, seeded and finely chopped, to taste

accompaniments

Poached prawns (shrimp), squid or chicken breasts, cooked pork or duck, thin omelette cut into strips, blanched or steamed vegetables, crispy fried sliced French shallots (eschalots), spring onions (scallions) thinly sliced on an angle, coriander (cilantro) leaves and finely chopped stems, crispy fried fresh ginger, diced silken tofu, toasted sesame seeds, salted peanuts, finely chopped chilli, sesame oil, **GF** fish sauce, **GF** soy sauce and **GF** tamari.

combine all ingredients in a slow cooker (see note) and cook on high for 3 hours or on low for 6 hours. Stir about every 30 minutes during cooking time. The congee is done when the rice dissolves into a thick, creamy porridge-like consistency. You may need to add more water/stock.

remove lime leaves and lemongrass before serving.

ladle congee into heated bowls and top with a combination of any of the accompaniments below.

note: If cooking congee in a stockpot, bring to the boil and immediately turn down to a simmer. Cook gently for about 2 hours. Stir congee occasionally to prevent sticking.

SAVOURY SECRET
Poach prawns (shrimp), squid or chicken in the congee just before serving. The chicken will take longer to poach than the prawns and squid. When chicken is cooked, slice it on an angle to serve.

cauliflower soup with cumin & parmesan croutons

This is a winter warmer soup that is full of flavour and comfort. The croutons add texture and taste great.

SERVES 4

cauliflower soup

60 g (2¼ oz) unsalted butter

1 large onion, finely chopped

1 garlic clove, crushed

1 teaspoon cumin seeds

2 bay leaves

500 g (1 lb 2 oz) cauliflower, broken into small florets

200 g (7 oz) all-purpose potatoes, peeled and diced

750 ml (26 fl oz/3 cups) **GF** chicken stock

250 ml (9 fl oz/1 cup) milk

80 ml (2½ fl oz/⅓ cup) pouring (whipping) cream

cumin & parmesan croutons

4 thick slices **GF** bread, crusts removed

20–40 g (¾–1½ oz) unsalted butter, melted

35 g (1¼ oz) finely grated parmesan cheese

1 teaspoon cumin seeds

lightly grease a baking tray.

cauliflower soup

heat butter in a large saucepan or small stockpot over medium heat. Add onion and cook until softened. Add garlic and cumin seeds and cook for 30 seconds, then add bay leaves, cauliflower, potato, stock and milk. Season with salt and freshly ground black pepper. Simmer for about 1 hour or until vegetables are well softened.

purée soup with cream in a food processor until smooth.

cumin & parmesan croutons

brush both sides of bread with butter and cut into 1.5 cm (⅝ inch) cubes.

combine parmesan and cumin seeds in a large bowl. Add bread cubes and toss to coat. Place in a single layer on the prepared baking tray. Sprinkle with some of the parmesan and cumin seed mixture remaining in the bowl.

preheat a grill (broiler) to high heat and toast croutons for 2–3 minutes until golden brown. Turn croutons, sprinkle with remaining parmesan and cumin seed mixture and cook until golden.

serve soup in heated bowls, topped with cumin & parmesan croutons.

jerusalem artichoke soup with seared scallops

Jerusalem artichokes are knobbly and have a delicate earthy flavour. This soup is extremely easy to prepare and may be made several days in advance. The scallops add a touch of elegance but are optional.

SERVES 4

seared scallops

60 ml (2 fl oz/¼ cup) olive oil

2 teaspoons finely chopped flat-leaf (Italian) parsley

12 scallops, cleaned, roe removed and discarded, and scallops drained on paper towel

soup

juice of 1 lemon

330 g (11½ oz) Jerusalem artichokes

250 g (9 oz) all-purpose potatoes, such as desiree

20 g (¾ oz) unsalted butter

1 celery stalk, finely chopped

1 leek, white part only, trimmed, rinsed well and thinly sliced

2 bay leaves

1 garlic clove, crushed

750 ml (26 fl oz/3 cups) **GF** chicken stock

white pepper, to taste

80 ml (2½ fl oz/⅓ cup) pouring (whipping) cream

olive oil, to drizzle (optional)

combine olive oil and parsley in a bowl. Add scallops and turn to coat. Marinate in refrigerator for up to 2 hours. Remove from refrigerator 30 minutes before cooking.

fill a medium-sized bowl with water and add lemon juice. Peel artichokes, slice thinly and place in lemon water. Do the same with potatoes.

melt butter in a large saucepan over medium heat. Add celery, leek and bay leaves and cook gently for 5 minutes. Add garlic and cook briefly.

drain artichokes and potatoes very well, add to the pan and stir for 1–2 minutes. Add stock, season well with salt and white pepper and simmer for 35 minutes or until vegetables are soft. Remove bay leaves.

purée soup with cream in a food processor until smooth. Do this in batches. Return soup to cleaned saucepan. Reheat soup to serve.

heat a frying pan over medium–high heat. Season scallops with salt and cook without disturbing for 60–90 seconds or until golden, turn and briefly cook other side. The scallops should feel springy to touch. Drain on paper towel.

serve soup in heated bowls. Place three scallops on top of each bowl of soup and drizzle with olive oil, if desired, to finish.

SAVOURY SECRETS

For a smoother silken-textured soup, pass the soup through a fine sieve after puréeing. Use a spoon or spatula to help push the purée through.

Substitute prawns (shrimp) or lobster for the scallops.

Soup may be frozen.

peasant soup

This is one of my favourite weekend soups as it's more like a meal than a starter. Peasant soup is so thick you can almost eat it with a fork! And it's great for using up all the vegetables in your refrigerator.

SERVES 8

1 tablespoon olive oil

75 g (2¾ oz) lean **GF** bacon
(about 4 slices), diced

1 onion, diced

1 leek, white part only, trimmed, rinsed well
and diced

2 garlic cloves, crushed

6 button or Swiss brown mushrooms, wiped
over with a damp paper towel and sliced

1 red capsicum (pepper), seeded, membrane
removed and diced

1 celery stalk, diced

2 carrots, diced

10 green beans, trimmed and cut into small
pieces or use 1 zucchini (courgette)

1 parsnip, diced

1 all-purpose potato, such as desiree, peeled
and diced

2 bay leaves

2 teaspoons dried oregano

2 x 400 g (14 oz) tins chopped tomatoes

1 tablespoon **GF** tomato paste (concentrated
purée)

1 litre (35 fl oz/4 cups) **GF** chicken or
GF vegetable stock (you may need a
little more)

400 g (14 oz) tin cannellini beans, drained
and rinsed

15 g (½ oz/½ cup) chopped flat-leaf (Italian)
parsley or a combination of herbs

parmesan cheese, grated or shaved, to finish

heat oil in a large 8–10 litre stockpot over medium–high heat and sauté bacon, onion and leek for 3 minutes, add garlic and sauté briefly before adding remaining fresh vegetables, bay leaves and oregano. Season with salt and freshly ground black pepper. Cook for a further 3–4 minutes.

add tomato, tomato paste and stock and cook until vegetables are tender.

add cannellini beans and herbs and simmer for a further 10 minutes.

serve soup in heated bowls topped with parmesan.

SAVOURY SECRETS

Omit bacon to make a vegetarian soup.

To vary the soup, add 1 **GF** chorizo sausage, diced and lightly pan-fried.

You can also add 1 cup cooked rice or **GF** macaroni or small shell **GF** pasta. Pasta tends to break up if soup is reheated. I find it best to add cooked pasta just before serving.

Another ideas is to add 1 cup diced chicken breast. Poach gently in the soup towards the end of cooking time.

simple borscht soup with sour cream & cucumber

This thick soup with its glorious crimson colour can be eaten hot or cold.

SERVES 6

4–6 beetroot (beets), trimmed and rinsed very well

1 tablespoon olive oil

1 onion, finely chopped

1 carrot, grated

1 celery stalk, finely chopped

2 garlic cloves, crushed

400 g (14 oz) tin chopped tomatoes

1 **GF** stock cube, chicken or vegetable flavour

1 tablespoon balsamic vinegar

15 g (½ oz/¼ cup) fresh dill, chopped or a combination of mint, parsley and basil

sour cream or crème fraîche, to serve

1 Lebanese (short) cucumber, peeled, seeded and diced

dill fronds, extra, to serve

place beetroot in a large saucepan and cover with approximately 1 litre (35 fl oz/4 cups) of water, then partially cover with a lid and cook over medium heat for 1 hour or until tender. Skim foam from cooking liquid as necessary.

strain the crimson-coloured liquid using a fine sieve and reserve the liquid. Rinse saucepan.

peel beetroot when they have cooled. To avoid staining your hands, wear latex gloves. Grate beetroot coarsely and set aside.

heat oil in a saucepan over medium heat and sauté onion, carrot, celery and garlic until softened.

add grated beetroot, reserved liquid, tomato, crumbled stock cube and vinegar and continue to cook for 5 minutes.

remove 500 ml (17 fl oz/2 cups) soup and purée with a stick blender or in a food processor. Return purée to soup and stir.

add herbs and season to taste. Chill if serving soup cold.

serve with a dollop of sour cream, cucumber and extra dill.

SAVOURY SECRETS

To vary the soup, serve topped with **GF** Greek-style yoghurt combined with **GF** prepared horseradish to taste.

Do not throw the beetroot leaves away as they are edible. Rinse well and use in salads or a stir-fry.

summer consommé

This recipe is based on Chipilin consommé, a soup that my husband and I ate on Christmas Day in Antigua, Guatemala. It looks very festive and can be eaten hot or cold. I have substituted baby spinach leaves for chipilin, the leafy vegetable traditionally used in this dish.

SERVES 4

1.5 litres (52 fl oz/6 cups) reduced **chicken stock** (see page 196)

1 cup baby English spinach leaves, cut into chiffonnade*

1 large avocado, finely diced

4 small perfectly ripe tomatoes, seeded and cut into small dice

zest of 2 limes, finely grated and reserve 1½ tablespoons juice

place stock in a saucepan over high heat and bring to the boil.

heat bowls if serving consommé hot and place a small mound of spinach in each bowl.

place avocado and tomato around the spinach.

add lime zest and juice to the stock just before serving.

ladle stock gently over spinach, avocado and tomato and serve immediately.

SAVOURY SECRET
The term chiffonnade* means to finely shred. To do this, stack six spinach leaves one on top of the other, roll the leaves tightly and finely slice. For this recipe, I slice through the chiffonnade lengthways so it is easy to eat.

asian-style omelette with vermicelli & ponzu sauce

At home we tend to have brunch instead of breakfast on weekends so I'm often looking for new ways to play with ingredients to keep it interesting. This recipe came about because we had leftover vermicelli noodles in the refrigerator.

SERVES 2

ponzu sauce

1 tablespoon **GF** tamari

1 tablespoon lemon or lime juice, strained

1 tablespoon fresh orange juice, strained

1 spring onion (scallion), thinly sliced on an angle

¼ teaspoon **GF** wasabi paste*, or to taste

1 teaspoon soft brown sugar

½ teaspoon sesame oil

1 red chilli, seeded and finely chopped, to taste (optional)

omelette

60 g (2¼ oz) **GF** rice vermicelli noodles

15 g (½ oz/½ cup) coriander (cilantro) leaves, rinsed well and dried on paper towel

2 spring onions (scallions), thinly sliced on an angle

4 x 60 g (2¼ oz) eggs

3 teaspoons fresh orange juice

1 teaspoon sesame oil

1 teaspoon bran or vegetable oil

10 g (¼ oz) unsalted butter

whisk ingredients for the ponzu sauce together with 2 teaspoons of water in a small bowl and set aside.

place vermicelli in a bowl and cover with 750 ml (26 fl oz/3 cups) boiling water and leave for 10 minutes to soften. Use a fork to separate noodles. Drain vermicelli, spread them on a clean tea towel (dish towel) and roll up to remove excess water.

combine vermicelli, coriander leaves and spring onion in a bowl and set aside.

break eggs into a bowl, add orange juice and whisk together.

heat oils and butter in a non-stick frying pan over medium heat. Add vermicelli mixture and spread it to the edge of the pan.

pour egg mixture over and cook undisturbed for 4–5 minutes. Loosen around the edge of the omelette with a spatula. Slide omelette out of pan on to a plate, cover with the frying pan and invert omelette back into pan. Cook for a further 2–3 minutes until done. Insert a small sharp knife into the omelette. The egg should be set, not runny.

slide omelette out of pan onto a board and cut into wedges. Serve the sauce separately in small individual dishes, if you wish.

SAVOURY SECRETS

Wasabi paste* is available in supermarkets and Asian grocery stores.

This omelette is delicious eaten cold. It is great to take on a picnic as you would a frittata.

Ponzu sauce can be used as a dipping sauce with other Asian-style food. It is also terrific with silken tofu, stir-fried vegetables and noodles or fish.

market mushrooms with garlic bread fingers

It is important to use a variety of mushrooms in this recipe for both taste and texture. Dark mushrooms have more flavour than pale varieties. This is a simple starter, breakfast dish or Sunday night dinner.

SERVES 2

market mushrooms

20 g (¾ oz) unsalted butter

1 tablespoon olive oil

50 g (1¾ oz) French shallots (eschalots), thinly sliced or use ½ a small red onion

1 garlic clove, crushed

350 g (12 oz) mixed mushrooms, include enoki, shiitake, Swiss brown and button mushrooms, wiped over with a damp paper towel, cut in half, thick slices or wedges

zest of 1 lemon, finely grated

125 ml (4 fl oz/½ cup) **GF** chicken or **GF** beef stock

2 tablespoons finely chopped flat-leaf (Italian) parsley

1 tablespoon pouring (whipping) cream

garlic bread fingers

1 tablespoon olive oil

1 garlic clove, crushed

1 teaspoon finely chopped lemon thyme

4 slices **GF** bread, crusts removed and cut into 2 or 3 fingers, depending on size of bread

additional ingredients

crème fraîche or sour cream, to serve (optional)

extra chopped flat-leaf (Italian) parsley, to serve

for the market mushrooms

heat butter and oil in a large non-stick frying pan over medium heat. A risotto pan works well. Add shallots and garlic and cook until softened. Do not brown.

turn up heat and add mushrooms. Cook for about 5 minutes or until mushrooms have softened. Do this in several batches if necessary.

stir in lemon zest, stock and parsley. Season with salt and freshly ground black pepper. Cook for 1 minute, add cream and boil to reduce and thicken slightly. Set aside while you prepare the garlic bread fingers.

for the garlic bread fingers

preheat the grill (broiler) to high.

combine olive oil, garlic and thyme in a small screw-top jar and shake well. Brush both sides of bread fingers and grill each side until golden.

serve market mushrooms with garlic bread fingers, a dollop of crème fraîche, if desired, and parsley.

serving suggestion
Serve with grilled or barbecued steaks, soft or grilled polenta, pasta or rice.

pizza with a dash of panache

I owe this recipe to my friend, foodie Fi. Together we created a pizza recipe that has the crisp base, light bready texture and mouth-watering aroma of a traditional pizza.

SERVES 4

fine (one-minute) instant polenta, to sprinkle

white rice flour, for dusting

1 teaspoon sugar

250 ml (9 fl oz/1 cup) warm water

16 g (½ oz) **GF** instant dried yeast

180 g (6½ oz) white rice flour

85 g (3 oz) potato flour

55 g (2 oz) tapioca flour

65 g (2½ oz) gluten substitute (Orgran GfG)*

25 g (1 oz) **GF** full-cream dried milk powder

1½ teaspoons **GF** baking powder

1 teaspoon salt

1 tablespoon extra virgin olive oil

1 x 60 g (2¼ oz) egg

toppings

Blanched thinly sliced potato, sliced **GF** chorizo sausage, sliced **roasted red capsicum** (page 164), mozzarella and basil pesto (page 115).

red onion & fennel confit (page 162), blanched thinly sliced pumpkin (winter squash), blue cheese and served with rocket (arugula) (optional).

Brush pizza base with a mixture of crushed garlic and olive oil and bake as above. Top cooked pizza with smoked salmon or ocean trout, goat's curd, thinly sliced **preserved lemon** (page 202), capers and dill. Do not bake the topping in this instance.

sprinkle oven trays with fine (one-minute) instant polenta.

preheat oven to 200°C (400°F/Gas 6).

place sugar, 150 ml (5 fl oz) of the warm water and yeast together in a small mixing bowl, stirring gently to combine. Leave to stand for 10 minutes or until the mixture becomes light, foamy and bubbles appear.

sift dry ingredients together and place in a food processor.

whisk together extra virgin olive oil and egg, then add to food processor, processing until combined. Add yeast mixture, again processing until combined. The mixture will still look rough and crumbly at this stage. To bring the mixture together, turn the food processor on and add the remaining warm water through the feed tube until the mixture comes together as a ball.

lightly dust a work surface with rice flour and gently knead dough for 2–3 minutes until dough is no longer sticky and becomes smooth. Place dough in a lightly oiled mixing bowl, cover with plastic wrap and leave in a warm, draught-free place until the dough has doubled in size. This will vary in time depending on the warmth of the room and may take up to 1 hour.

divide the dough into 4 or 8 even-sized pieces, depending on the pizza size you want. Use the heel of your hand to flatten and shape the dough. Place on prepared oven trays and add toppings of your choice, leaving a 2 cm (¾ inch) border around the edge of the dough.

bake for 18–20 minutes or until pizza is cooked to your liking.

SAVOURY SECRETS

Gluten substitute (Orgran GfG)* is available in supermarkets.

The pizza dough makes excellent **focaccia.** Once the dough has doubled in size, knock it back by gently flattening the dough and pushing some air out of it. Place the flattened dough in a large deep oiled cake tin and cover with plastic wrap again. Allow dough to rise again by half its size. Remove plastic wrap and press your fingertips into the dough to make indentations. Drizzle generously with olive oil, sprinkle with rosemary and sea salt. Bake in a preheated oven at 200°C (400°F/Gas 6) for 30 minutes or until golden and crispy.

preserved lemon panna cotta with smoked ocean trout

This is a fairly rich and ever-so-sexy starter. I recommend you follow it with just a light main course. You can cheat with commercial gluten-free whole-egg mayonnaise or prepare my own recipe.

SERVES 4 OR DOUBLE THE QUANTITY
FOR 6 LARGE SERVES

grape seed oil, for greasing

60 ml (2 fl oz/¼ cup) milk

60 ml (2 fl oz/¼ cup) pouring (whipping) cream

2 teaspoons gelatine powder

2 tablespoons warm water

60 g (2¼ oz/¼ cup) **GF** Greek-style yoghurt

60 g (2¼ oz/¼ cup) **GF** whole-egg mayonnaise*

20 g (¾ oz) preserved lemon**, pulp discarded, rind rinsed and finely chopped

2 teaspoons lemon or lime juice

1 teaspoon **GF** prepared horseradish

a pinch of sweet paprika

2 Lebanese (short) cucumbers

4–8 smoked ocean trout slices, depending on how generous you want to be

lemon zest, thinly sliced (optional)

dill sprigs (optional)

olive oil, to drizzle (optional)

lightly grease 4 x 125 ml (4 fl oz/½ cup) ramekins or dariole moulds, or use Chinese teacups, with grape seed oil.

place milk and cream in a microwave-safe container and heat on high for 90 seconds. Alternatively heat in a saucepan over low heat until warm.

sprinkle gelatine over warm water and allow to soak in for 30 seconds. Microwave on medium for 30–40 seconds or until dissolved. Stir well. Alternatively, follow directions on packet to dissolve gelatine.

combine gelatine with warmed milk and cream mixture. Add yoghurt and mayonnaise and stir well. Add preserved lemon, lemon juice, horseradish and paprika and stir again to combine. Pour mixture into ramekins or dariole moulds filling each about two-thirds full. Cover with plastic wrap and place in refrigerator to set.

remove panna cotta from refrigerator 30 minutes before serving. To remove panna cotta from ramekins, run a small thin-bladed knife around the edge of the custard and invert onto plates.

slice cucumbers into long ribbons using a vegetable peeler. Try to leave an edge of green skin on some ribbons. Stop peeling when you reach the seeds. Discard the seeds.

serve panna cotta with ocean trout, a small mound of cucumber ribbons, lemon zest and garnish with dill.

SAVOURY SECRETS

GF whole-egg mayonnaise* is available in supermarkets or prepare **whole-egg mayonnaise** (page 201).

Preserved lemons** are available in supermarkets or prepare **preserved lemons** (page 202).

Substitute smoked salmon, prawns or lobster for the smoked ocean trout.

smoked salmon on toast with wasabi mayonnaise

Quantities for this recipe will vary according to the size of bread slices used and how generous you are with the salmon. The wasabi mayonnaise takes the place of butter.

SERVES 2

wasabi mayonnaise

125 g (4½ oz/½ cup) **whole-egg mayonnaise** (page 201)*

2 teaspoons **GF** wasabi paste**, or to taste

zest of 2 limes, finely grated and 1–2 teaspoons juice

additional ingredients

4 slices **GF** multi-grain bread

4–8 slices smoked salmon

2 spring onions (scallions), thinly sliced on an angle, to serve

zest of 1 lime, thinly sliced to finish

place mayonnaise in a bowl and add wasabi paste, zest and juice. Stir well to blend. The mayonnaise will take on a lovely green hue. Taste and adjust if necessary.

preheat grill (broiler) to high and toast bread on both sides until golden.

place salmon on toast and spoon a dollop of wasabi mayonnaise on top. Top with spring onion and lime zest, to finish.

SAVOURY SECRETS
Take a short cut and purchase **GF** whole-egg mayonnaise*.

GF wasabi paste** is available in supermarkets.

To vary the recipe, add a few slices of avocado or cucumber ribbons on top of the wasabi mayonnaise and serve with a lime wedge.

Wasabi mayonnaise goes well with barbecued prawns, squid, fish and chicken.

spanish-style omelette with potato, red capsicum & chorizo

This omelette is like a frittata and is perfect for brunch, lunch or when baked in the oven can be cut into cubes to serve as finger food.

SERVES 4

450 g (1 lb) cooked new potatoes, peeled sliced or quartered

200 g (7 oz) **roasted red capsicum** (page 164), cut into 1 cm (½ inch) strips or pan-fry one large sliced red capsicum (pepper)

1 **GF** chorizo sausage, thinly sliced

1 teaspoon olive oil

1 red onion, thinly sliced

4 x 60g (2¼ oz) eggs

60 ml (2 fl oz/¼ cup) pouring (whipping) cream

1 tablespoon fresh orange juice

2 tablespoons roughly chopped flat-leaf (Italian) parsley

1 teaspoon sweet smoked paprika

2 teaspoons unsalted butter

place potato and capsicum in a large bowl.

heat a medium-sized non-stick frying pan and cook chorizo slices until lightly browned. Drain on paper towel then add to potato and capsicum.

add oil to pan and sauté onion over low–medium heat for about 5 minutes or until well softened. Add to large bowl and gently combine with potato, capsicum and chorizo.

place eggs, cream, orange juice, parsley and paprika in a separate bowl and whisk to combine.

melt butter in a large non-stick frying pan over medium heat. Add potato and capsicum mixture and spread it to the edge of the pan. Pour over egg mixture.

turn heat down to low. As eggs begin to set around the edge of the pan, use a spatula to drag the cooked egg in just a few centimetres (about an inch), allowing the uncooked mixture to flow out towards the edge of the pan. It will take about 20 minutes for the omelette to set as it is cooked gently. The omelette will still be wobbly in the centre so pop it under a low–medium grill (broiler) until firm. Do not have the grill heat too fierce or the omelette will burn. If necessary, cover frying pan handle with foil to protect it from burning.

serve omelette cut into wedges.

SAVOURY SECRETS

If the potato is hot when combined with capsicum, chorizo and onion, the egg mixture will begin to cook immediately, so cooking time will be less than if potato is cold or at room temperature.

The omelette can also be baked in a 23 x 23 x 5 cm (9 x 9 x 2 inch) greased and baking paper-lined ceramic ovenproof dish. Preheat oven to 170°C (325°F/Gas 3) and bake for 20–25 minutes or until set.

MAINS

baked fennel & leek risotto with fish

This is a shortcut to the traditional method of making risotto on the stovetop—and equally delicious.

SERVES 4

2 teaspoons chopped fennel fronds

2 teaspoons finely grated lemon zest

40 g (1½ oz) unsalted butter, melted

4 white fish fillets (about 200 g/7 oz each), such as whiting or garfish

risotto

750 ml (26 fl oz/3 cups) **GF** fish, **GF** chicken or **GF** vegetable stock

1 tablespoon olive oil

20 g (¾ oz) unsalted butter

1 leek, white part only, trimmed, rinsed well and thinly sliced

2 small fennel bulbs, trimmed and finely sliced (reserve fronds for finishing the risotto)

1 garlic clove, crushed

2 bay leaves

zest of 2 lemons, finely grated and reserve 2 tablespoons juice

220 g (7¾ oz/1 cup) arborio rice

125 ml (4 fl oz/½ cup) dry white wine

40 g (1½ oz) grated parmesan cheese

choose a large deep flameproof casserole dish or risotto pan with a lid.

preheat oven to 180°C (350°F/Gas 4).

combine fennel fronds, zest and butter. Brush both sides of fillets with butter mixture and place on a foil-lined baking tray. Set aside while you cook the risotto.

place the stock in a saucepan over medium–high heat and bring to a simmer.

heat oil and butter in the casserole dish over medium–low heat and sauté leek and fennel for 3–4 minutes. Add garlic, bay leaves and lemon zest and cook briefly. Add rice and stir for about 2 minutes, or until well coated.

add wine and boil rapidly until wine has almost evaporated. Add stock, season with salt and freshly ground black pepper and stir to combine. Cover with lid and transfer to the oven.

bake for about 15 minutes until rice is *al dente*. Add reserved lemon juice and parmesan, stir to combine, then cover and leave to stand while you cook the fish.

preheat grill (broiler) to high. Place fish under the grill until just cooked through. There is no need to turn the fish if the fillets are thin.

serve risotto with grilled fish and fennel fronds.

serving suggestions
Serve with baby English spinach leaves.

SAVOURY SECRETS
You can replace the grilled fish with small pieces of raw fish, crabmeat, prawns (shrimp) or chicken, added to the risotto towards the end of cooking time. The heat from the risotto will cook the meat. Stir in some fresh dill to serve.

For a creamy (soupy) risotto, add 20 g (¾ oz) extra butter and a little more stock at the end of cooking time.

beer batter fish & best potato wedges

It is such a treat for people with coeliac disease to be able to eat fish and chips that taste even better than those bought at the local fish and chip shop. This batter is light and crispy. Prepare the wedges first so that they are ready by the time you have cooked the fish.

SERVES 4

700 g (1 lb 9 oz) flathead fillets, each cut into 4 fingers (sticks)

best potato wedges

55 g (2 oz/½ cup) **GF** breadcrumbs*

25 g (1 oz/¼ cup) grated parmesan cheese

1 kg (2 lb 4 oz) potatoes, such as desiree, sebago or kipfler (fingerling), cut into wedges

2 tablespoons melted butter

2 tablespoons oil

beer batter

45 g (1¾ oz/¼ cup) white rice flour

30 g (1 oz/¼ cup) pure maize cornflour (cornstarch)

35 g (1¼ oz/⅓ cup) besan (chickpea flour)

1 teaspoon **GF** baking powder

½ teaspoon salt

1 x 60 g (2¼ oz) egg, lightly beaten

125 ml (4 fl oz/½ cup) **GF** beer (I use O'Brien Pale Ale)

additional ingredients

bran, canola or vegetable oil, for shallow-frying fish

pure maize cornflour (cornstarch), extra, for coating fish

lemon wedges, to serve

line two baking trays with baking paper. One baking tray is for the wedges. Place a wire rack on the second tray.

preheat oven to 200°C (400°F/Gas 6).

combine breadcrumbs and parmesan. Season with salt and freshly ground black pepper. Brush potato wedges with combined butter and oil and sprinkle crumb mixture all over. Place on the baking tray. Bake for 30 minutes until crisp and golden.

reduce the oven temperature to 170°C (325°F/Gas 3) so it is ready for the batches of fish to be kept warm after frying.

sift flours, baking powder and salt into a bowl. Make a well in the centre and add egg. Whisk gently to incorporate and gradually add beer. Whisk well to combine.

heat oil for frying in a medium–sized frying pan.

dust fish with extra cornflour to coat. This is so the batter sticks to the fish. Dip a piece of fish in the batter and then drag it up the side of the bowl to remove excess batter. Place gently in oil and repeat with remaining fish. Cook a few pieces at a time for 2–3 minutes or until cooked. Place fish on the prepared wire rack and keep warm in the oven until all of the fish is cooked.

serve fish and wedges with lemon and/or **quick tartare sauce** (page 201).

SAVOURY SECRETS

GF breadcrumbs* see **cook's tips — bread** (page 210).

To make **sumac squid** follow beer batter recipe above and add 1 teaspoon sumac*. Dust squid pieces with pure maize cornflour (cornstarch) then dip in sumac batter and fry. Serve with **cheat's lime mayonnaise** (page 201).

Sumac* is a Lebanese lemon-scented spice with a rich earthy colour. It goes well with fish, squid, chicken and lamb, sprinkled over hummus or in pilaff.

crunchy crusted snapper with beurre blanc

You can prepare the snapper completely ahead of time so that it's just a matter of popping it in the oven when you are ready to eat. Remember to remove the snapper from the refrigerator 30 minutes before baking. Beurre blanc is a delicious white butter sauce.

SERVES 4

4 skinless snapper fillets or other thick-fleshed fish fillets

1–2 tablespoons melted butter, to brush fish

olive oil, to drizzle

crunch

110 g (3¾ oz/1 cup) **GF** breadcrumbs*

40 g (1½ oz/¼ cup) blanched almonds or other nuts, chopped

60 g (2¼ oz) unsalted butter, softened

1½ tablespoons chopped herbs, use a mixture of parsley with dill or tarragon

zest of 1 lemon, lime or grapefruit, finely grated

beurre blanc

60 ml (2 fl oz/¼ cup) white wine vinegar

125 ml (4 fl oz/½ cup) dry white wine

50 g (1¾ oz) French shallots (eschalots), peeled and very finely chopped

1 tablespoon pouring (whipping) cream

150 g (5½ oz) cold unsalted butter, cut into small dice

line a baking tray with baking paper.

preheat oven to 200°C (400°F/Gas 6).

combine crunch ingredients in a bowl. Season with salt and freshly ground black pepper. Blend butter in with your fingers.

place snapper fillets on the baking tray and brush all sides lightly with melted butter. Press crunch on top of the fish and drizzle with a little olive oil.

bake snapper for about 10–12 minutes or until crunch is golden and snapper is cooked. Timing will depend on the thickness of the fish. Prepare sauce while fish is baking.

place vinegar, wine and shallots in a small saucepan, bring to the boil and reduce to 2 tablespoons. Strain reduction using a fine sieve pressing down on the solids to extract as much liquid as possible. Discard solids. Return liquid to saucepan, add cream and bring to the boil. Remove from the heat and whisk in butter, piece by piece, until sauce thickens. Do not reheat as sauce may split. Season with salt and white pepper. Serve warm with the snapper fillets.

serving suggestions
Serve with sautéed English spinach and a few baby vegetables.

SAVOURY SECRETS
GF breadcrumbs* see **cook's tips — bread** (page 210).

Serve beurre blanc with grilled fish, poultry, beef, lamb or steamed vegetables.

A squeeze of lemon juice may be added to the beurre blanc, if desired.

polenta, coconut & lime-coated fish

SERVES 4

4 flathead fillets, cut into even-sized thick fingers (sticks)

polenta, coconut & lime coating

90 g (3¼ oz) fine (one-minute) polenta

60 g (2¼ oz/½ cup) pure maize cornflour (cornstarch)

30 g (1 oz/½ cup) shredded coconut

zest of 2 limes, finely grated

additional ingredients

60 g (2¼ oz/½ cup) pure maize cornflour (cornstarch), extra

1 x 60 g (2¼ oz) egg

125 ml (4 fl oz/½ cup) whole milk

vegetable or bran oil, for shallow-frying

combine ingredients for the polenta, coconut & lime coating and set aside.

place extra cornflour on a plate.

make an egg wash by whisking egg and milk together in a shallow bowl.

place fish in cornflour and turn to coat both sides, shake off any excess. Dip in egg wash and then press coating ingredients on both sides. Place coated fish on a plate and refrigerate until required. Remove from refrigerator 30 minutes before cooking.

heat about 1 cm (½ inch) oil in a frying pan over medium heat. Cook fish in batches. Timing will depend on thickness of the fish. Wipe pan with paper towel after frying each batch of fish. Add more oil as necessary. Keep the fish warm in a preheated oven at 170°C (325°F/Gas 3).

serving suggestions
Serve with **hot & spicy corn & avocado salsa** (page 146), baby English spinach leaves and crème fraîche.

SAVOURY SECRET
Substitute chicken tenderloins for the fish fillets.

sesame-glazed salmon with pickled ginger rice

The combination of sesame oil, ginger and cumin teamed with pickled ginger rice makes this one of my favourite fish recipes. It is cooked at a low temperature in the oven so remains perfectly moist. I love the sweet taste of pickled ginger and it looks so pretty with the contrasting black nigella seeds in the rice.

SERVES 4

4 x 175 g (6 oz) salmon fillets, skin on

olive oil, for brushing fish before cooking

marinade for the salmon

1 tablespoon ginger syrup, from a jar or vacuum pack of pink pickled ginger*, chopped

1 tablespoon sesame oil

2 teaspoons **GF** tamari

1 tablespoon grated fresh ginger

1 tablespoon soft brown sugar

1–2 garlic cloves, crushed

zest of 1 lime, finely grated

2 teaspoons ground cumin

pickled ginger rice

300 g (10½ oz/1½ cups) long-grain white rice

2 makrut (kaffir lime) leaves

50 g (1¾ oz/⅓ cup) pink pickled ginger*, or to taste, thinly sliced

1 tablespoon nigella seeds**, or use black sesame seeds

line a baking tray with baking paper.

preheat oven to 120°C (235°F/Gas ½).

combine marinade ingredients and rub over salmon. Marinate in the refrigerator for 1–2 hours. Remove from refrigerator 30 minutes before cooking.

cook rice according to packet instructions, adding lime leaves to the water. They will give the rice a wonderful aromatic flavour. When rice is cooked and drained, stir through pickled ginger and nigella seeds. Set aside.

heat a chargrill pan over medium–high heat. Remove salmon from marinade and reserve marinade. Dab salmon with paper towel to remove excess marinade. Brush salmon with olive oil and grill for 1 minute each side. Transfer salmon to baking tray and drizzle with reserved marinade.

bake salmon for 12 minutes or until cooked to your liking.

serve salmon with marinade from the baking tray, pickled ginger rice and **asian greens & cucumber salad** (page 130), omitting the radish.

SAVOURY SECRETS

Pink pickled ginger* is available from supermarkets in jars or vacuum packs.

Nigella seeds** are available from health food and speciality stores. They are jet black in colour, have an aromatic, smoky flavour and are popular in Middle Eastern and Indian cookery.

To mould hot pickled ginger rice, place rice in a ramekin, cup or dariole mould and press it in gently. Invert the container on a dinner plate. Remove container and repeat for remaining serves.

Rice can be prepared ahead of time and reheated in the microwave to serve.

sumac fish with preserved lemon & caper salsa

The zing of lemon is hard to beat when it comes to fish. Here I have doubled up on the flavour with sumac.

4 snapper fillets, blue-eye or other white-fleshed fish, skin off (about 200 g/7 oz each)

3 teaspoons olive oil

1 tablespoon sumac*

zest of 1 lemon or lime, finely grated

10 g (¼ oz) unsalted butter

2 teaspoons olive oil, extra

1 quantity **preserved lemon & caper salsa** (page 148)

brush fish fillets with olive oil.

mix sumac and lemon zest together and sprinkle it over the fish.

heat butter and extra olive oil in a large frying pan over medium heat and cook fish for 2–3 minutes on each side or until cooked to your liking. Remove fish to a warm plate. Set aside to rest for a few minutes.

serve fish with preserved lemon & caper salsa.

serving suggestions
Serve with potato purée with cooked lentils folded through.

SAVOURY SECRETS
Sumac* is a Lebanese lemon-scented spice with a rich earthy colour. It goes well with fish, squid, chicken and lamb, sprinkled over hummus or in pilaff.

Substitute chicken tenderloins for the fish fillets.

chicken in red wine with mushrooms & shallots

My daughter Kate is an excellent cook. This year for my birthday dinner she cooked her version of coq au vin. It was such a hit that it has become another family favourite.

SERVES 6

6 chicken leg quarters (leg and thigh portion)

pure maize cornflour (cornstarch), for dusting

40 g (1½ oz) unsalted butter

250 g (9 oz) French shallots (eschalots), covered with boiling water for 5 minutes, drained and peeled or use 12 spring onions (shallots), trimmed and chopped

1 carrot, diced

1 celery stalk, diced

250 g (9 oz) Swiss brown mushrooms, halved or quartered, depending on size

165 g (5¾ oz) **GF** pancetta or **GF** bacon, diced

2 garlic cloves, crushed

60 ml (2 fl oz/¼ cup) brandy

300 ml (10½ fl oz) good-quality dry red wine

300 ml (10½ fl oz) **GF** chicken stock

2 tablespoons **GF** tomato paste (concentrated purée)

2 bay leaves

6 sprigs each flat-leaf (Italian) parsley and thyme, tied together in a bundle with cooking twine

2 strips of lemon peel, pith removed

choose a large deep flameproof casserole dish with a tight-fitting lid.

preheat oven to 160°C (315°F/Gas 2–3).

season chicken with freshly ground black pepper and dust lightly all over with cornflour.

melt butter in the casserole dish over medium heat and brown chicken. Do this in batches. Remove chicken to a large bowl. Add shallots, carrot, celery and mushrooms to dish and cook until shallots are lightly browned. Add pancetta and garlic and cook briefly. Remove to the large bowl with the chicken.

add brandy to dish and cook until it has almost evaporated. Add wine and bring to the boil. Stir and scrape up any brown residue on the base of the dish. Add stock and tomato paste and stir to blend.

add chicken and vegetable mixture, bay leaves, herbs and lemon peel. Bring to a simmer. Place a piece of baking paper on top and press down lightly. This is called a cartouche. It prevents evaporation and keeps the casserole from drying out. Cover with casserole dish lid and bake in the oven for 1–1½ hours or until chicken is very tender.

cool see **cook's tips — cooling** (page 211) and refrigerate casserole. When fat sets, remove and discard with spoon. Warm casserole on the stovetop, as the sauce will have jellied. As soon as the jelly melts, remove the chicken and reserve. Boil sauce rapidly to reduce. Return chicken to sauce and reheat to serve.

serving suggestions
Serve with parsnip and potato purée, **crisp parsnip ribbons or 'spaghetti'** (page 154) and a green vegetable.

SAVOURY SECRETS
This recipe can be cooked a day or two in advance and reheated to serve.
You can make a cornflour paste to thicken the sauce if you wish.
Add 1 tablespoon drained capers to the recipe towards the end of cooking time.

chicken poached in ginger broth

You can feel this broth doing you good! The broth sits comfortably as a starter or main course.
I prefer to use a well-reduced home-made chicken stock for the broth.

SERVES 4 AS A MAIN
OR 8 AS A STARTER

4 skinless, boneless chicken breasts, trimmed of fat and sinew

ginger broth

1.5 litres (52 fl oz/6 cups) well-reduced **GF** chicken stock

3 makrut (kaffir lime) leaves

30 g (1 oz) fresh ginger, peeled and sliced

2 lemongrass stems, bruised

4 star anise

2 garlic cloves, sliced

1 red chilli, seeded and sliced on an angle, to taste

additional ingredients

200 g (7 oz) rice stick noodles

1 red chilli, extra, seeded and thinly sliced, to finish

GF soy sauce and/or **GF** fish sauce, served separately

accompaniments

Crispy fried shredded ginger, coriander (cilantro) leaves, Vietnamese mint, lime wedges, or thinly sliced red capsicum (pepper) poached in the broth. Wok-fried or blanched bok choy (pak choy).

place ingredients for the ginger broth in a large saucepan or small stockpot and bring to the boil. Reduce heat to medium and simmer for 15 minutes. Strain ginger broth through a fine sieve, into a large bowl. Reserve star anise (optional) and discard remaining solids. Return broth to saucepan.

poach chicken breasts very gently in the broth for about 5 minutes or until cooked through.

place rice noodles in a saucepan of boiling water and cook for 3–4 minutes until softened. Do not overcook noodles as they tend to break up. Cook the noodles while the chicken is poaching.

remove chicken from broth to a chopping board and thinly slice on an angle. To avoid burning your hands wear latex gloves.

drain rice noodles well and divide between heated bowls. Place sliced chicken on top of noodles. Strain the ginger broth again over the chicken and noodles. Finish with extra chilli and one star anise per serve, if desired. Choose from any of the accompaniments below.

chicken tagine with lemon & olives

Exotically flavoured with spices, preserved lemon and olives, this easy recipe will bring the sunny taste of Morocco to your table.

SERVES 4

2 tablespoons olive oil

1 large onion, thinly sliced

1 garlic clove, crushed

1½ tablespoons **GF** tagine spice mix*

8 skinless, boneless chicken thighs, trimmed of fat and sinew

250 ml (9 fl oz/1 cup) **GF** chicken stock

zest of 1 orange, finely grated and reserve 80 ml (2½ fl oz/⅓ cup) orange juice, strained

2 ripe tomatoes, cored and finely chopped

20 g (¾ oz) preserved lemon**, pulp discarded, rind rinsed and finely chopped

85 g (3 oz/½ cup) stuffed green olives***

coriander (cilantro) leaves, to finish

toasted almonds or pine nuts, to finish

choose a large frying pan with a lid or a risotto pan.

heat 1 tablespoon oil in a large frying pan and sauté onion over medium–low heat for 5 minutes. Add garlic and cook briefly. Remove onions and garlic to a bowl and set aside.

combine spice mix and freshly ground black pepper and pat all over chicken. Roll chicken up and secure with toothpicks or cooking twine.

add remaining oil to the frying pan and brown chicken rolls. Add onion and garlic mixture, stock, zest and juice, tomato and preserved lemon. Cover frying pan with lid, reduce heat to low and simmer for 10 minutes. Turn chicken and cook for another 10 minutes or until cooked through.

remove chicken to a large plate and cover loosely with foil to keep warm. Remove toothpicks or twine.

boil sauce uncovered for 5–7 minutes to reduce. Add olives and return chicken to sauce, then simmer to reheat. Finish with coriander and nuts.

serving suggestions

Serve with **saffron pilaff with vermicelli** (page 205). A side dish of grilled eggplant (aubergine) or **roasted red capsicum** (page 164) works well too.

SAVOURY SECRETS

Tagine spice mix* is a Moroccan spice blend available in some supermarkets, health food and speciality stores.

Chickpeas make a terrific addition to this recipe.

Preserved lemons** are available in supermarkets or prepare **preserved lemons** (page 202).

You could use chicken pieces and allow longer cooking time.

Use almond or pimento stuffed green olives***.

duck breasts with saffron ginger glaze

The honey and saffron give the glaze a beautiful golden hue.

SERVES 4

4 boneless duck breast fillets, skin on

2 teaspoons **GF** Chinese five-spice

saffron ginger glaze

90 g (3¼ oz/¼ cup) runny honey

60 ml (2 fl oz/¼ cup) dry sherry

125 ml (4 fl oz/½ cup) **GF** chicken stock

1 tablespoon lemon or lime juice

1 small red onion, finely chopped

30 g (1 oz) fresh ginger, peeled
and finely chopped

2 star anise, plus 2 extra to serve

1 garlic clove, sliced

1 red chilli, seeded and sliced
on an angle, to taste

generous pinch of saffron threads

choose a frying pan that is suitable for both stovetop cooking and oven use. Alternatively, line a baking tray with baking paper.

preheat oven to 200°C (400°F/Gas 6).

score fat on fillets in a criss-cross pattern using a thin-bladed knife. Season with salt and freshly ground black pepper. Sprinkle five-spice all over duck fillets and set aside.

combine ingredients for the saffron ginger glaze in a small saucepan and simmer for 15 minutes. Remove star anise and reserve. Strain glaze through a fine sieve and press down on the onions to extract as much juice as possible. Discard the solids. Return glaze to saucepan and bring to the boil, then lower heat to achieve a rapid simmer. Reduce glaze to 125 ml (4 fl oz/½ cup). This will take about 10 minutes. Add all four star anise to the glaze and set aside.

heat a frying pan over medium heat and cook duck fillets, skin side down, for 3 minutes. Do not add any fat to the pan as scoring the skin helps to render the fat. Turn fillets over and cook for 1 minute. Pour off fat from the pan and reserve. See savoury secrets below.

transfer duck to the oven or place on a baking tray. Bake for 6–8 minutes until done to your liking. Remove from the oven to a warm plate and rest for 5 minutes. If duck skin is not crispy, pop under the grill (broiler), preheated to high, for 1 minute just before serving.

slice duck fillets on an angle. To avoid burning your hands wear latex gloves. Serve with glaze and one star anise per serve.

serving suggestions

Serve with steamed bok choy (pak choy), snake (yard-long) beans or whole green beans. Rice cooked by absorption method with 2 makrut (kaffir lime) leaves added to the water or **GF** chicken stock. Place cooked rice in ramekin or dariole mould and turn out on to plates. Top rice with spring onions (scallions) sliced on an angle.

SAVOURY SECRETS

The glaze can be prepared several days in advance and refrigerated.

The glaze can be served with chicken, pork or quail.

The reserved duck fat can be used for roasting potatoes.

gremolata–stuffed chicken

This Italian salsa is traditionally served sprinkled over dishes such as osso buco, but here I've played with the ingredients to create a moist, tangy stuffing for chicken. It is also delicious served cold.

SERVES 4

4 boneless chicken breasts, skin on,
or 4 chicken leg quarters (leg and thigh
portion), skin on

gremolata stuffing

20 g (¾ oz/1 cup) flat-leaf (Italian) parsley,
roughly chopped

1 tablespoon baby capers, rinsed well if salted
and drained on paper towel

2 garlic cloves, crushed

30 g (1 oz) preserved lemon*, pulp discarded,
rind rinsed and finely chopped

30 g (1 oz) unsalted butter, softened

additional ingredients

10 g (¼ oz) unsalted butter, melted

2 teaspoons bran or vegetable oil

line a baking tray with baking paper.

preheat oven to 180°C (350°F/Gas 4).

place ingredients for the gremolata stuffing in a bowl and rub butter in using your fingers.

separate skin from chicken by pushing your fingers or rolling the handle of a wooden spoon, under the skin to lift and separate it from the flesh. Spread a quarter of the stuffing under the skin of each breast or leg quarter. Pat the skin back to its original shape. Brush chicken liberally with additional combined butter and oil. Season with freshly ground black pepper.

heat a frying pan over medium–high heat and brown chicken skin side down, then turn chicken and brown the other side. Transfer chicken to the baking tray and pour over any remaining butter mixture from the pan. Bake chicken breasts for about 12 minutes or leg quarters for 30 minutes or until cooked through.

remove chicken from oven and cover loosely with foil. Rest chicken for a few minutes before serving. Slice each breast on an angle in half or in slices. Serve chicken leg quarters whole. Drizzle with pan juices to finish.

serving suggestions
Serve with **cheesy soft polenta** (page 203), roasted vine-ripened truss tomatoes and grilled zucchini (courgette).

SAVOURY SECRETS
Preserved lemons* are available in supermarkets or prepare **preserved lemons** (page 202).

Chicken can be prepared in advance and refrigerated until required. Remove from refrigerator 30 minutes before cooking.

To make **whole chicken with gremolata stuffing** use your fingers or roll the handle of a wooden spoon under the skin to lift and separate it from the flesh. Push stuffing under the skin, down the legs and thighs and under the breast. Roast chicken in the oven at 200°C (400°F/Gas 6) for 1–1½ hours depending on the size of the chicken. The stuffing keeps the chicken beautifully moist.

icky sticky chicken legs

This is a very easy recipe that can be prepared several hours before eating. The chicken legs make delicious picnic food. They can be baked in the oven or grilled on the barbecue.

SERVES 4

8–10 large free-range chicken legs

icky sticky marinade

1 garlic clove, crushed

60 ml (2 fl oz/¼ cup) bran or vegetable oil

2 teaspoons sesame oil

1 tablespoon grated fresh ginger

zest of 1 lime or lemon, finely grated and reserved juice

1 tablespoon runny honey or soft brown sugar

1 tablespoon **GF** tamari or **GF** worcestershire sauce

1 tablespoon **GF** sweet chilli sauce

2 tablespoons **GF** tomato sauce (ketchup)

1 tablespoon Japanese rice vinegar

2 teaspoons ground cumin

additional ingredient

sesame seeds, to sprinkle

line a shallow baking dish with baking paper.

preheat oven to 180°C (350°F/Gas 4).

combine ingredients for the marinade in a glass dish or stainless steel bowl. Add the chicken and marinate in the refrigerator for 1½–2 hours or overnight. Alternatively, place chicken and marinade in a large zip-lock plastic bag to marinate. Remove from refrigerator 30 minutes before cooking.

remove chicken legs from marinade and place in the baking dish. Reserve marinade. Sprinkle legs with sesame seeds and bake for 35–45 minutes or until cooked through. Baste with reserved marinade once or twice during cooking. You can add any remaining marinade to the baking dish towards the end of cooking time. Allow marinade to bubble in the dish and serve it over the chicken.

serving suggestions
Serve with rice or rice noodles and **asian greens & cucumber salad** (page 130), if serving chicken hot, or **sweet & spicy mango salsa** (page 148), if serving chicken cold.

SAVOURY SECRETS
Substitute chicken wings or drummettes for the chicken legs. The marinade (omit tomato sauce) works very well with quail too.

To barbecue the chicken legs, preheat barbecue grill to low–medium heat and brush with oil. Grill chicken legs, turning often so that they do not burn. Baste with marinade. Cooking time will depend on the size of the chicken legs. Boil any remaining marinade in a small saucepan or heat in the microwave and serve it over the chicken. Add a little water if necessary.

orange marmalade duck ragout

This is a wonderful, rich and satisfying way to enjoy duck.

SERVES 4–6

4–6 duck leg quarters (leg and thigh portion)

1 large onion, finely diced

1 carrot, finely diced

1 celery stalk, finely diced

6 Swiss brown mushrooms, thickly sliced

2 garlic cloves, crushed

500 ml (17 fl oz/2 cups) red wine

500 ml (17 fl oz/2 cups) **GF** chicken stock

2 tablespoons **GF** tomato paste
(concentrated purée)

1 tablespoon orange marmalade

zest of 1 orange, finely grated and
reserved juice

2 bay leaves

6 juniper berries*, lightly crushed

1 tablespoon thyme leaves

flat-leaf (Italian) parsley, to finish

heat a large flameproof casserole dish over medium heat. Season duck with freshly ground black pepper and cook for 3 minutes. Turn legs over and cook for a further 3 minutes. Do this in batches if necessary. Remove duck from casserole dish and set aside briefly.

add onion, carrot, celery and mushrooms to the dish and cook, stirring for 3 minutes. Add garlic and cook briefly. There will be fat residue from searing the duck so do not add more.

add wine and bring to the boil. Add stock, tomato paste, marmalade, zest and juice, bay leaves, juniper berries, thyme and duck. Reduce heat to low and simmer partially covered for 1½–2 hours until meat is almost falling off the bone.

remove duck to a plate and cool. Remove meat from the bones. Discard skin and bones. Cover duck meat and place in refrigerator.

cool sauce see **cook's tips — cooling** (page 210) and refrigerate. When fat sets remove and discard it. Boil sauce rapidly over high heat to reduce by half. Skim froth from the surface and discard.

return reserved duck meat to sauce and fold in gently. Reheat to serve.

serving suggestions
Serve over buttered **GF** fettucine sprinkled with parsley or with **cheesy soft polenta** (page 203) and a side of **green beans with hazelnut oil & roasted hazelnuts** (page 156).

SAVOURY SECRETS
Juniper berries* are the fruit of an evergreen tree. When ripe and dried they impart a distinctive sweet-sharp taste. Juniper berries are available in the spice section in most supermarkets.

The ragout can be prepared a day or two in advance and refrigerated or may be frozen.

To vary ragout, add some cooked brown lentils after reducing the sauce.

To make **slow cooked lamb shanks** substitute 4–6 French-trimmed lamb shanks for the duck leg quarters. Brown shanks in butter and oil and prepare sauce as above. Preheat oven to 150°C (300°F/Gas 2) and bake shanks in a covered casserole dish for 2–3 hours until tender. Cool shanks and discard fat. Remove shanks and reduce sauce by boiling rapidly over high heat. Return shanks to sauce and reheat. Serve with potato or parsnip purée and a green vegetable.

prosciutto–wrapped chicken with leek & ricotta

I love anything that can be prepared in advance and then baked off with a minimum of fuss.

SERVES 4

10 g (¼ oz) unsalted butter

2 teaspoons olive oil, plus extra, for brushing

4 boneless, skinless chicken breasts, tenderloin removed to use in another recipe or freeze

2 small leeks, white part only, trimmed, rinsed well and thinly sliced

1 garlic clove, crushed

90 g (3¼ oz/⅓ cup) ricotta cheese, drained in a paper towel-lined colander

35 g (1¼ oz/⅓ cup) grated parmesan cheese

2 tablespoons chopped flat-leaf (Italian) parsley

8 thin prosciutto slices (4 slices may be enough depending on how long and wide they are)

line a baking tray with baking paper.

preheat oven to 180°C (350°F/Gas 4).

heat butter and oil in a large frying pan over high heat. Season chicken with freshly ground black pepper and brown quickly on both sides. Remove from pan to a plate.

sauté leeks in the same frying pan over medium heat until softened. Add garlic and cook briefly. Cool a little.

combine ricotta, parmesan and parsley with cooled leeks.

cut a pocket about 5 cm (2 inches) deep along the side of each chicken breast with a sharp knife. Fill each pocket with a quarter of ricotta filling. Roll meat back over the filling to close the pocket.

wrap each fillet in prosciutto, brush with extra olive oil and place on the baking tray.

bake for 12–15 minutes or until cooked through. Allow chicken to rest for a few minutes before serving whole or slice each fillet in half on an angle.

serving suggestions
Serve with pan juices or **easy tomato sauce** (page 200), sautéed mushrooms and baby English spinach leaves.

SAVOURY SECRET
Chicken may be prepared up to 8 hours in advance and refrigerated. Remove from refrigerator 30 minutes before baking.

sage & citrus quail

Ask your butcher to bone or butterfly the quail if you are not up to it. Place finger bowls on the table if quail is not boned. You can also prepare **last minute chicken** using the marinade.

SERVES 4

6 quail, boned or butterflied (see note)

marinade

60 ml (2 fl oz/¼ cup) olive oil, plus extra, for brushing

1 tablespoon brandy

2 teaspoons runny honey

1 garlic clove, crushed

zest of 1 small orange, finely grated and reserved juice

zest of 1 lime or lemon, finely grated and reserve 1 tablespoon juice

3 teaspoons finely chopped sage leaves, or use rosemary or thyme

combine ingredients for the marinade in a glass or stainless steel bowl. Reserve 2 tablespoons of marinade to drizzle over quail after cooking.

marinate quail and place in the refrigerator for 1–1½ hours. Turn once during this time.

preheat barbecue to medium. Brush grill with oil. Barbecue quail skin side down for 3–4 minutes. Brush with marinade then turn and cook other side for 3 minutes or until cooked through. Boned quail don't take long to cook at all. Allow 4–5 minutes each side if quail is not boned.

remove quail to a warm plate, drizzle with reserved marinade, cover loosely with foil and rest for 5–10 minutes before serving.

note: Use poultry shears or kitchen scissors to cut either side of the backbone. Discard backbone. Open quail out and press down to crack bones so they lie flat. Rinse and pat dry with paper towel. Cut the quail in half if you wish.

serving suggestions
Serve with marinade and **blood orange, fennel & olive salad** (page 138) or **lemon & parsley potatoes** (page 161).

SAVOURY SECRET
To make **last minute chicken** you require 4 boneless, skinless chicken breasts. Slice each chicken breast into three thin escalopes or place them one at a time in a large freezer bag then pound thick end lightly with a meat mallet or rolling pin to flatten to 1 cm (½ inch) thickness. Cut each pounded chicken breast into three even-sized pieces. Prepare the marinade above, reserving several tablespoons to drizzle over the chicken after cooking. Marinate chicken for about ½–1 hour. Preheat barbecue to medium. Brush grill with oil and barbecue chicken for about 3 minutes on each side or until cooked through.

spatchcock with craisin & pistachio stuffing

I prepared this stuffing for my Christmas turkey and loved it so much I now use it to stuff spatchcock (poussin) too. The spatchcock are quite large when stuffed. You can serve half per person if you wish. Use an electric knife to cut the spatchcock in half.

SERVES 4–8

4 x 500 g (1 lb 2 oz) spatchcock (poussin), cavity rinsed and wiped with paper towel

craisin & pistachio stuffing

1 tablespoon olive oil

1 small onion, finely diced

1 celery stalk, finely diced

1 **GF** bacon slice, chopped

1 garlic clove, crushed

25 g (1 oz) unsalted butter

165 g (5¾ oz/1½ cups) **GF** breadcrumbs*

zest of 1 orange, finely grated

30 g (1 oz) preserved lemon**, pulp discarded, rind rinsed and finely chopped

30 g (1 oz/¼ cup) flat-leaf (Italian) parsley, chopped

1 tablespoon fresh thyme leaves

80 g (2¾ oz/⅔ cup) craisins***

40 g (1½ oz/¼ cup) unsalted pistachio nuts

1 x 60 g (2¼ oz) egg, lightly beaten

additional ingredients

extra olive oil and melted butter, combined

1–2 onions, cut into 5 mm (¼ inch) slices

pan sauce

½ teaspoon **GF** mustard powder

60 ml (2 fl oz/¼ cup) white wine

125 ml (4 fl oz/½ cup) **GF** chicken stock

a splash of pouring (whipping) cream

grease the base of a large flameproof baking dish.

preheat oven to 200°C (400°F/Gas 6).

heat oil in a frying pan over medium heat, sauté onion and celery until softened. Add bacon and garlic and cook briefly. Add butter to the pan to melt. Set aside.

combine breadcrumbs, zest, lemon, herbs, craisins and pistachios in a large bowl and stir in onion and bacon mixture. Add egg to bind and season with freshly ground black pepper. Cool stuffing before spooning into spatchcock cavities. Tie legs together with cooking twine. Brush spatchcock with extra olive oil and butter mixture and season with freshly ground black pepper.

place sliced onions in the baking dish and rest spatchcock on top. Bake for 45 minutes or until cooked through. Test with a skewer by inserting it in the thickest part of the thigh. The juices should run clear. Transfer the spatchcock to a large warm plate, cover with foil and leave to rest.

spoon excess fat from baking dish. Place over medium heat. Stir in mustard, deglaze dish with wine and bring to the boil. Stir and scrape up any brown residue on the base. Add stock and cook for several minutes. Strain contents through a fine sieve over a bowl, pressing down on the onions to extract as much flavour as possible. Discard onions. Return sauce to dish or a small saucepan. Warm sauce and add cream to finish. Transfer sauce to a jug to serve.

serving suggestions

Serve with **roughed-up roasted potatoes** (page 166) and snow peas (mangetout) or asparagus. Pan sauce and/or cranberry sauce.

SAVOURY SECRETS

GF breadcrumbs* see **cook's tips — bread** (page 210).

Preserved lemons** are available in supermarkets or prepare **preserved lemons** (page 202).

Craisins*** (sweetened dried cranberries) are available in supermarkets.

Make extra stuffing, bake in a loaf (bar) tin and enjoy with leftover turkey or chicken in a salad or sandwich with cranberry sauce and/or **GF** mayonnaise.

spicy chicken

This quick and versatile recipe can be served with a summer salad. It also makes a wonderful meal at cooler times of the year.

SERVES 4

1 tablespoon sesame oil

1 tablespoon bran or grape seed oil

1 garlic clove, crushed

500 g (1 lb 2 oz) chicken tenderloins, trimmed of fat or sinew

1 teaspoon fennel seeds, crushed to a fine powder using a mortar and pestle

1 teaspoon cumin seeds, crushed to a fine powder using a mortar and pestle

1 teaspoon **GF** Chinese five-spice

1 teaspoon ground ginger

¼ teaspoon ground chilli powder or flakes, to taste

½ teaspoon sugar

additional ingredients

20 g (¾ oz) unsalted butter

1 tablespoon bran or grape seed oil

combine sesame oil, bran oil and garlic in a bowl. Add chicken and stir thoroughly to coat.

place chicken on a large plate in a single layer.

combine fennel, cumin, Chinese five-spice, ginger, chilli, sugar, salt and pepper to taste in a small bowl. Pat spice mixture on both sides of the chicken.

heat a frying pan over medium heat and add half the butter and oil. Cook chicken in two batches. The tenderloins will take about 2 minutes on each side to cook. Remove to a warm plate. Wipe pan with paper towel. Add remaining butter and oil and cook second batch of chicken.

serving suggestions

Serve with **baby spinach & mango salad with lime drizzle** (page 134). The meal can be plated individually or served on one large platter if you are catering for a crowd. Alternatively, prepare **saffron pilaff with vermicelli** (page 205). When pilaff is cooked, stir in some sliced dried apricots, pistachio nuts and chopped coriander (cilantro) leaves to finish. You can serve a side bowl of **GF** Greek-style yoghurt combined with 1 teaspoon sumac too, if you wish.

beef & mushroom hotpot

This rich hotpot meal is the ultimate comfort food on a cold winter's night. I just love the aroma that comes from the oven while it is cooking, slow and steady. It really gets my taste buds excited.

SERVES 4–6

1 tablespoon olive oil

20 g (¾ oz) unsalted butter (you may need a little more)

2 onions, cut into quarters

200 g (7 oz) Swiss brown mushrooms, halved or quartered, depending on size

2 garlic cloves, crushed

1.5 kg (3 lb 5 oz) beef bolar (see note), chuck or rump, in one piece, tied with cooking twine

500 ml (17 fl oz/2 cups) full-bodied red wine

2 tablespoons **GF** dijon mustard

1½ tablespoons redcurrant jelly

1 tablespoon **GF** worcestershire sauce

1 **GF** chicken stock cube, crumbled

6 thyme sprigs

2 bay leaves

7 g (⅛ oz/¼ cup) roughly chopped flat-leaf (Italian) parsley

1 tablespoon pure maize cornflour (cornstarch), mixed with 2 tablespoons water, to thicken

choose a large deep flameproof casserole dish with a tight-fitting lid.

preheat oven to 150°C (300°F/Gas 2).

heat oil and butter in casserole dish over medium–low heat and sauté onions for 5 minutes. Add mushrooms and brown lightly. Add garlic and cook briefly. Remove vegetables to a large bowl and set aside.

season beef with freshly ground black pepper, place in the dish and brown well on all sides over high heat. Remove and add to vegetables.

add red wine to the dish and bring to the boil. Add mustard, redcurrant jelly, worcestershire sauce, stock cube, thyme, bay leaves, vegetables and beef. Cover with lid. Place dish in the oven and bake for 2–3 hours until the beef is very tender, it should be just about falling apart. Turn beef after 1 hour and add half the parsley. When beef is cooked, remove it to a plate using a slotted spoon and cover loosely with foil. Strain sauce over a bowl, reserve vegetables and discard thyme and bay leaves. Rinse casserole dish.

cool sauce see **cook's tips — cooling** (page 211) and refrigerate. When fat sets remove and discard it. Return sauce to casserole dish. Place over high heat and bring to a rapid boil to reduce the sauce a little. Thicken sauce with the cornflour paste.

remove twine from beef. Cut off and discard any fat. Pull beef apart into chunks rather than slicing. Return beef and vegetables to dish and simmer gently to reheat.

serve hotpot sprinkled with remaining parsley.

note: Beef bolar is a large cut of meat which comes from the pointed end of the chuck blade. It is more tender than most other blade.

serving suggestions
Serve with boiled new potatoes tossed in melted butter and sprinkled with chives or celeriac purée and a green vegetable.

SAVOURY SECRETS
The hotpot may be cooked 2 days in advance.
Substitute quince paste, cut into small pieces, or honey, for the redcurrant jelly.
Substitute **GF** tamari for the **GF** worcestershire sauce.

chilli beef with guacamole salsa

Cocoa, chilli and red wine give this dish a delicious rich flavour. I always make this quantity so that I have leftovers for the freezer.

SERVES 8–10

1 quantity **guacamole salsa** (page 146)

chilli beef

1 tablespoon bran oil

2 onions, thinly sliced

1 red capsicum (pepper), seeded, membrane removed and diced

2 garlic cloves, crushed

1 hot chilli, finely chopped, to taste

1 kg (2 lb 4 oz) lean minced (ground) beef

125 ml (4 fl oz/½ cup) red wine

250 ml (9 fl oz/1 cup) **GF** chicken or **GF** beef stock

2 bay leaves

2 x 400 g (14 oz) tins chopped tomatoes

4 tablespoons **GF** tomato paste (concentrated purée)

2 teaspoons soft brown sugar

2 tablespoons unsweetened cocoa powder (I use Dutch cocoa)

2 tablespoons harissa paste*, or to taste

2 teaspoons mixed dried herbs

400 g (14 oz) tin red kidney beans, drained and rinsed

125 g (4½ oz) tin chickpeas, drained and rinsed

prepare guacamole salsa and set aside.

heat a large frying pan over medium heat. Add oil and sauté onions and capsicum until softened. Add garlic and chilli and cook briefly. Remove to a large bowl.

increase heat to high and brown beef in batches. Do not add too much beef at a time as it will stew rather than brown. Add browned beef to the onion and capsicum.

deglaze pan with wine and bring to the boil. Add stock, bay leaves, tomatoes, tomato paste, sugar, cocoa, harissa paste, herbs and the beef, onion and capsicum mixture. Bring to the boil then reduce heat to low and simmer for 40 minutes or until well reduced.

add red kidney beans and chickpeas and heat through to serve.

serving suggestions
Serve with guacamole salsa, sour cream and **chickpea flat bread** (page 14).

SAVOURY SECRETS
Harissa paste* is a traditional accompaniment to Tunisian dishes. It is a wonderful vibrant red, hot paste made with chilli. It is available in supermarkets and speciality stores.

If your children do not like whole beans, you can purée half the beans and stir in with the remainder so even if they pick out the beans they will still get some nutrients from the 'hidden' puréed beans!

crepe lasagne

Lasagne made with crepes makes a very nice change from the traditional lasagne pasta sheets. It is not as heavy on the tummy either. I've replaced béchamel sauce with layers of quick cheesy ricotta.

SERVES 6

1 quantity **herbed crepes** (page 207)

quick cheesy ricotta

750 g (1 lb 10 oz/3 cups) ricotta cheese, drained in a paper towel-lined colander

3 x 60 g (2¼ oz) eggs, lightly beaten

100 g (3½ oz/1 cup) grated parmesan cheese

bolognese sauce

1 tablespoon olive oil

1 onion, finely diced

1 carrot, grated

1 celery stalk, finely diced

1 red or green capsicum (pepper), seeded, membrane removed and finely diced

2 **GF** bacon slices, finely diced

1 or 2 garlic cloves, crushed

1 bay leaf

500 g (1 lb 2 oz) lean minced (ground) beef

200 ml (7 fl oz) red or white wine

400 g (14 oz) tin chopped tomatoes

2 tablespoons **GF** tomato paste (concentrated purée)

1 **GF** stock cube, crumbled

1 teaspoon sugar

1 teaspoon dried oregano

2 tablespoons chopped flat-leaf (Italian) parsley

additional ingredients

grated parmesan cheese, extra

freshly grated nutmeg, to finish

grease and line the base and side of a 24 cm (9½ inch) spring-form cake tin with baking paper.

preheat oven to 180°C (350°F/Gas 4).

prepare herbed crepes.

combine ricotta, eggs and parmesan in a bowl. Set aside.

heat oil in a frying pan over medium–low heat. Add onion, carrot, celery and capsicum and cook gently for 3 minutes. Add bacon, garlic and bay leaf and cook briefly. Transfer to a large bowl. Increase heat to high and add beef in batches, crumbling it into the pan. Use a fork to break it up. Do not overcrowd pan or the beef will stew instead of browning. When beef has browned, add to vegetable and bacon mixture. Repeat until you have browned all the beef.

add wine to the pan and bring to the boil. Stir and scrape any brown residue on the base of the pan. Add tomato, 250 ml (9 fl oz/1 cup) water, tomato paste, stock cube, sugar, herbs and beef mixture. Season with freshly ground black pepper. Simmer sauce for 35–40 minutes until well reduced. It is important for the sauce to be very firm to layer well in the crepes. Cool sauce.

place one crepe on the lined cake-tin base and spread with a quarter of the bolognese sauce. Top with a second crepe. Spread this crepe with a quarter of the quick cheesy ricotta and top with a third crepe. Continue to layer the lasagne until you have used all of the bolognese sauce, cheesy ricotta and crepes. Finish with a layer of cheesy ricotta and sprinkle with extra parmesan and nutmeg. Place the lined spring-form side around the crepe lasagne and secure. Place the crepe lasagne on a baking tray.

bake for about 1 hour until golden on top. Rest for 10 minutes before removing spring-form side. Cut into wedges, using a thin-bladed knife, to serve.

serving suggestions
Serve with a green salad, shaved parmesan and olives. Dress salad with olive oil and balsamic vinegar.

SAVOURY SECRETS
The herbed crepes and bolognese sauce can be made in advance and frozen.
The bolognese sauce can also be served over **GF** spaghetti.

greek beef or lamb kebabs

I spent two months travelling around the Greek Islands and ate my fair share of souvlaki. I still love kebabs as they are easy to prepare ahead of time and quick to barbecue.

SERVES 4

500 g (1 lb 2 oz) beef rump or boneless lamb loin, trimmed of fat and sinew and cut into 2.5 cm (1 inch) cubes

marinade

2 tablespoons olive oil, plus a little extra, to drizzle over kebabs before cooking

60 ml (2 fl oz/¼ cup) red wine

zest of 1 lemon, finely grated and reserve 1 tablespoon juice

1 small onion, very finely chopped

1–2 garlic cloves, crushed

1 tablespoon dried oregano, or use 1½ tablespoons finely chopped oregano or rosemary

2 bay leaves

vegetables

1 red onion, cut into six wedges and separated

1 red capsicum (pepper), seeded, membrane removed and cut into 2.5 cm (1 inch) pieces

1 green capsicum (pepper), seeded, membrane removed and cut into 2.5 cm (1 inch) pieces

16 button mushrooms, halved if large

soak eight bamboo skewers in water for 30 minutes (to prevent them from burning during cooking) or use metal skewers. Alternatively, use firm rosemary stems stripped of all but a few leaves at the top.

combine the marinade ingredients in a ceramic dish or stainless steel bowl. Marinate meat for 1–2 hours.

preheat the barbecue grill to medium–high.

thread marinated meat alternating with onion, capsicums and mushrooms onto the skewers.

drizzle extra oil over kebabs and barbecue for 2–3 minutes on each side or until done to your liking.

serving suggestions
Serve with steamed rice and a bowl of **GF** Greek-style yoghurt combined with crushed garlic and chopped mint.

SAVOURY SECRETS
To make **chicken kebabs** substitute white wine for the red wine in the marinade.

Omit the vegetables other than onion from the kebabs and make a **greek salad with a twist** to serve. Combine cherry tomatoes, baby English spinach, sliced marinated artichoke hearts (from a jar), crumbled feta cheese and black olives. Drizzle salad with olive oil and lemon juice.

herby lamb with lentils du puy

SERVES 4

60 ml (2 fl oz/¼ cup) olive oil

1–2 garlic cloves, crushed

12–16 French-trimmed lamb cutlets or 650 g (1 lb 7 oz) boneless lamb loin, trimmed of fat and sinew

herby lamb rub

zest of 2 lemons, finely grated

1½ tablespoons chopped mixed herbs, such as parsley, rosemary, thyme and oregano

1 teaspoon dried mixed herbs

1½ teaspoons ground cumin

lentils du puy

200 g (7 oz/1 cup) lentils du puy*, rinsed and checked for small stones

15 g (½ oz) unsalted butter

½ onion, finely chopped

1 celery stalk, finely chopped

1 small carrot, finely chopped

1 garlic clove, crushed

1 bay leaf

500 ml (17 fl oz/2 cups) **GF** chicken or **GF** vegetable stock

2 tablespoons chopped flat-leaf (Italian) parsley

additional ingredient

115 g (4 oz) soft goat's curd, to serve

combine oil and garlic in a small bowl and brush over lamb.

combine ingredients for the herby lamb rub. Pat over lamb and marinate for 1–3 hours or more.

place lentils in a large saucepan, cover with water and place over medium heat. Bring up to a simmer then drain immediately and reserve lentils. Rinse saucepan.

heat butter in the same saucepan over medium heat. Add onion, celery and carrot and sauté until softened. Add garlic and bay leaf and cook briefly then add stock and reserved lentils. Bring to the boil and reduce heat to low. Cover with lid and simmer for 35 minutes until lentils are tender. If stock has not been absorbed in this time, remove lid and continue to cook until stock is absorbed. Add parsley. Season with salt and freshly ground black pepper. Cover and set aside.

heat a chargrill pan or barbecue to medium–high. Cook lamb cutlets for 2–3 minutes each side or lamb loin for 3–4 minutes each side until cooked to your liking. Rest lamb, covered loosely with foil for 5 minutes. Slice lamb loin across the grain to serve.

serve lamb with lentils du puy and a dollop of goat's curd. Serve goat's curd separately if you wish.

serving suggestions
Serve with roasted carrots and/or chargrilled wedges of eggplant (aubergine) or zucchini (courgette). Drizzle a little **demi-glaze** (page 198) or vin cotto** on the plate.

SAVOURY SECRETS
The rub can be used with chicken, beef and lamb.

Lentils du puy* are from Le Puy-en-Velay in the Auvergne region of France. They are available in health food and speciality stores. Australian fine green lentils may be substituted for the lentils du puy. You can prepare the lentils in advance and reheat them in the microwave for 3 minutes on medium heat.

Cook extra lentils to use in **red capsicum & lentil potpies with feta crumble** recipe (page 124).

Vin cotto** is an Italian wine vinegar that is available in speciality stores.

italian meatloaf roll with tomato & capsicum sauce

This meatloaf roll looks impressive. It is excellent served cold too.

SERVES 6

tomato & capsicum sauce

2–3 ripe tomatoes, about 300 g (10½ oz) in total or use tin chopped tomatoes

2 teaspoons olive oil

125 g (4½ oz) roasted red capsicum (page 164), roughly chopped

125 ml (4 fl oz/½ cup) **GF** chicken stock

¼ teaspoon balsamic vinegar

meatloaf roll

250 g (9 oz/½ bunch) English spinach, trimmed and rinsed

2 teaspoons olive oil

1 onion, finely chopped

1 garlic clove, crushed

750 g (1 lb 10 oz) lean minced (ground) beef

115 g (4 oz) **GF** spicy salami, ground in a food processor or **GF** bacon, finely chopped

110 g (3¾ oz) **GF** breadcrumbs*

2 teaspoons dried mixed herbs

2 tablespoons chopped herbs, such as parsley, rosemary and/or oregano

1 x 60 g (2¼ oz) egg

6-8 prosciutto slices, depending on the width of the slices

100 g (3½ oz) semi-dried tomatoes

75 g (2¾ oz) pitted kalamata olives

1 tablespoon capers, rinsed well if salted and drained on paper towel

line a baking tray with baking paper.

score a cross in the base of each tomato using a sharp knife and blanch in boiling water for 30–60 seconds, peel then roughly chop. Heat oil in a frying pan and sauté tomato until soft. Add remaining ingredients and simmer for 5 minutes. Purée sauce in a food processor. Set aside.

blanch spinach in boiling water and refresh in cold water. Squeeze water from spinach and spread on a clean tea towel (dish towel). Roll spinach in tea towel to remove excess water. You should be left with approximately 150 g (5½ oz) blanched spinach leaves. Set aside.

heat oil in a small frying pan over medium heat and sauté onion until softened. Add garlic and cook briefly, then remove from the heat and cool.

combine onion and garlic with beef, salami, breadcrumbs, herbs and egg in a large bowl. Mix well.

tear a piece of freezer wrap or foil measuring approximately 46 x 33 cm (18 x 13 inches). Place prosciutto slices vertically, slightly overlapping along the freezer wrap or foil. Place meat mixture on top and shape by patting it down into a rectangle measuring approximately 32 x 24 cm (13 x 9½ inches).

spread spinach leaves down the centre of the mixture leaving a 5 cm (2 inch) border along each long edge. Place semi-dried tomatoes, olives and capers in rows down the centre of the spinach.

preheat oven to 180°C (350°F/Gas 4).

roll the mixture into a long meatloaf roll using the freezer wrap or foil as a guide and twist ends. Place meatloaf roll in the refrigerator to firm for 30 minutes. Remove from refrigerator 30 minutes before baking. You can prepare meatloaf up to this stage several hours ahead of cooking.

remove freezer wrap or foil from meatloaf roll and carefully place seam-side down on prepared baking tray. Bake for 40–45 minutes or until cooked through.

serve meatloaf roll in thick slices with warm tomato & capsicum sauce and baked fennel or eggplant (aubergine).

slow-cooked lamb with raisins & pine nuts

SERVES 6

1.5 kg (3 lb 5 oz) boned lamb leg, cut into 5 cm (2 inch) cubes

zest of 3 oranges, finely grated and reserve 310 ml (10¾ fl oz/1¼ cups) fresh orange juice, strained

1 tablespoon chopped thyme or rosemary

2 bay leaves

2 garlic cloves, crushed

2 tablespoons seeded tamarind pulp concentrate*

30 g (1 oz) unsalted butter

1½ tablespoons olive oil

1 large onion, diced

3 teaspoons za'atar**

2 teaspoons ground cumin

2 teaspoons ground coriander

chilli powder or flakes, to taste (optional)

125 ml (4 fl oz/½ cup) red wine

1 tablespoon dry sherry

1 **GF** chicken stock cube, crumbled

3 tomatoes, diced or use 200 g (7 oz) tin chopped tomatoes

20 g (¾ oz) preserved lemon***, pulp discarded, rind rinsed and finely chopped

60 g (2¼ oz/½ cup) seedless raisins

1 tablespoon pure maize cornflour (cornstarch) mixed with 2 tablespoons water (optional)

4 tablespoons pine nuts, toasted, to finish

preheat oven to 150°C (300°F/Gas 2).

combine lamb, zest, juice, thyme, bay leaves and garlic in a glass bowl. Marinate for at least 2 hours or preferably overnight. Drain lamb in a colander set over a bowl and reserve marinade. Pat lamb dry with paper towel.

soak tamarind in 125 ml (4 fl oz/½ cup) hot water. Use your fingers or a fork to break up the pulp. Strain, reserve the purée and discard fibres. Set aside.

heat 1 teaspoon each of butter and oil in a large frying pan over medium heat, sauté onion until softened, add spices and cook briefly. Remove mixture to a large casserole dish. Add another teaspoon each of butter and oil to the pan. Season lamb with freshly ground black pepper and brown in batches. Do not overcrowd the pan or the meat will stew. Add lamb to casserole dish after browning each batch.

add wine, sherry and tamarind to frying pan and bring to the boil. Stir and scrape any brown residue from the base of the pan. Add reserved marinade, crumbled stock cube, tomato and preserved lemon. Pour mixture over lamb. Gently press lamb into the liquid which should just cover the lamb, if not add a little water. Place a piece of baking paper on top and press down lightly to keep the casserole from drying out. Cover dish with lid, place in oven and cook for 1½ hours. Add raisins and continue to cook for 30–60 minutes until lamb is very tender.

cool see **cook's tips — cooling** (page 211) and refrigerate casserole. When fat sets, remove and discard it. Remove lamb from liquid and reserve. Place casserole dish over high heat, bring to a rapid boil and reduce liquid to about 2 cups. Stir in cornflour paste to thicken, if desired. Return lamb to sauce and simmer to reheat. Serve with toasted pine nuts.

serving suggestions

Serve with quinoa or rice and/or **baked pumpkin with sweet smoked paprika** (page 150).

SAVOURY SECRETS

Tamarind pulp concentrate* or wet tamarind is available in blocks with or without seeds. It comes from a tropical tree native to Africa and is used to flavour sauces, impart acidity to dishes and also as a thickening agent. It is available from Middle Eastern or Asian grocery stores.

Za'atar** is a traditional Middle Eastern spice blend of thyme, sesame seeds and sumac. It is available from supermarkets, Middle Eastern or Asian grocery stores.

Preserved lemons*** are available in supermarkets or prepare **preserved lemons** (page 202).

basil pesto pasta with 'no-mess' poached eggs

This recipe is quick, easy and very satisfying. You can make the poached eggs in the traditional way or try my 'no-mess' method. The added bonus is that you have only to wipe the saucepan dry!

SERVES 4

basil pesto

100 g (3½ oz) basil leaves

2 garlic cloves, crushed

2 tablespoons pine nuts

80 ml (2½ fl oz/⅓ cup) olive oil

25 g (1 oz/¼ cup) grated parmesan cheese

30 g (1 oz/¼ cup) grated Romano cheese

additional ingredients

350 g (12 oz) **GF** spaghetti or other **GF** pasta

shaved parmesan cheese, to serve

baby basil leaves, to serve

'no-mess' poached eggs

4 x 60 g (2¼ oz) eggs, at room temperature

olive oil, to brush

blanch basil quickly in boiling water. Refresh immediately in cold water. Place on paper towel or a clean tea towel (dish towel) and gently dab to remove excess water. Blanching basil stops the pesto from discolouring.

place basil, garlic and pine nuts in a food processor. With motor running, slowly add oil through the feed tube. Add cheeses and continue to process until ingredients are blended.

cook pasta in boiling salted water until *al dente*. While pasta is cooking, prepare poached eggs.

place a large saucepan three-quarters full with water over medium–high heat and bring up to a simmer.

tear a piece of microwave-safe plastic wrap approximately 36 cm (14¼ inches) long and place it on your work surface. Brush a little olive oil in the centre of the plastic and then place it loosely over a small dish. Break one egg into it, gather up the corners of the plastic, remove from dish and twist plastic into a rope. Loop it through to tie a knot close to the egg. Alternatively, twist the rope and use cooking twine to tie a knot close to the egg. Repeat with remaining eggs.

place eggs in simmering water and cook for about 4 minutes. Lift the eggs with a slotted spoon to feel if they are cooked to your liking. Remove eggs from water and rest on paper towel. Leave eggs to sit briefly while you strain the pasta.

strain pasta, reserving 1–2 tablespoons of cooking liquid to add to the pesto. Fold pesto through pasta and divide between heated bowls. To serve the eggs, cut just under the knot with scissors and peel away the plastic. Use a spoon to lift poached eggs and place one on top of each serve of pasta. You can pierce the egg with a knife and let the yolk ooze over the pasta, if you wish. Serve with shaved parmesan and a baby basil leaves.

SAVOURY SECRETS
To vary the pesto, use equal quantities of basil, rocket and parsley.

If serving 'no-mess' poached eggs on toast for breakfast, add a drizzle of truffle oil once you have broken the egg into the plastic wrap. Twist the plastic, tie the 'rope' and poach as above.

herbed crepes with spinach & ricotta

These crepes are lovely to serve for brunch or lunch.

MAKES 8 CREPES

1 quantity **herbed crepes** (page 207)

spinach and ricotta filling

500 g (1 lb 2 oz/1 bunch) English spinach, trimmed and rinsed well

1 teaspoon olive oil

10 g (¼ oz) unsalted butter

1 small onion, finely chopped, or use 4 spring onions (scallions), thinly sliced

1 garlic clove, crushed

500 g (1 lb 2 oz/2 cups) ricotta cheese, drained in a paper towel-lined colander, reserving 60 g (2¼ oz/¼ cup) to spread on top of filled crepes.

½ teaspoon freshly grated nutmeg

additional ingredients

grated parmesan cheese and cheddar cheese, to finish

freshly grated nutmeg, extra, to finish

pine nuts, toasted, to serve (optional)

line a baking tray with baking paper.

preheat oven to 180°C (350°F/Gas 4).

prepare herbed crepes. If you have made and frozen the crepes in advance, defrost and then microwave each one for 10 seconds on high heat to soften before filling, otherwise they may crack.

blanch spinach in boiling water and then refresh in cold water. Lightly squeeze water from spinach and spread it on a clean tea towel (dish towel). Roll spinach in tea towel (dish towel) to remove excess water. You should be left with approximately 300 g (10½ oz) blanched spinach. Chop spinach roughly and set aside.

heat oil and butter in a frying pan over medium heat and sauté the onion for about 5 minutes or until soft. Add garlic and cook briefly.

combine ricotta, spinach, onion and garlic mixture and nutmeg.

place crepes on a work surface. Divide spinach and ricotta mixture between crepes and place it in the centre. Make a 7 x 7 cm (2¾ x 2¾ inch) square with the mixture. Fold crepe over to enclose. Place crepe parcel seam-side down on baking tray. Spread reserved ricotta on top and sprinkle with combined parmesan, cheddar cheese and nutmeg.

bake for about 15 minutes until cheese is bubbling and golden.

serve crepes with toasted pine nuts scattered over, if desired.

serving suggestions

Serve with **easy tomato sauce** (page 200) with fresh basil, or a side of salad greens, mushrooms and olives drizzled with olive oil and balsamic vinegar.

SAVOURY SECRETS

Herbed crepes with spinach & ricotta can be prepared in advance and frozen or prepared a day in advance, covered with plastic wrap and refrigerated. Defrost if frozen and remove from refrigerator 30 minutes before baking.

mediterranean vegetable & ricotta gratin

Although this gratin is a vegetarian meal it can also be served with grilled chicken, beef and lamb.

SERVES 4–6

80 ml (2½ fl oz/⅓ cup) olive oil

1 garlic clove, crushed

500 g (1 lb 2 oz) eggplants (aubergines), cut into 5 mm (¼ inch) slices

400 g (14 oz) butternut pumpkin (squash), seeded, peeled and cut into 5 mm (¼ inch) slices

350 g (12 oz) zucchini (courgettes), cut into long thin strips

400 g (14 oz) red capsicums (peppers)

500 g (1 lb 2 oz/2 cups) ricotta cheese, drained in a paper towel-lined colander

100 g (3½ oz/1 cup) grated parmesan cheese

2 x 60 g (2¼ oz) eggs

30 g (1 oz/1 cup) flat-leaf (Italian) parsley, roughly chopped

additional ingredients

50 g (1¾ oz/½ cup) grated parmesan cheese, extra

50 g (1¾ oz) **GF** breadcrumbs*

olive oil, extra, to drizzle

line 2 or 3 baking trays with baking paper.

grease a 23 x 23 x 5 cm (9 x 9 x 2 inch) square ovenproof dish or similar size rectangular dish and line the base with baking paper.

preheat oven to 180°C (350°F/Gas 4).

combine oil with garlic and brush both sides of vegetable slices lightly with the oil.

place prepared eggplant, pumpkin and zucchini on baking trays and bake for 15–20 minutes or until tender. Roast capsicum until skin blisters and blackens. Cool capsicum, peel, remove seeds and membranes and open out flat.

combine ricotta, parmesan, eggs and parsley in a large bowl and season with freshly ground black pepper.

place a layer of eggplant in the base of the ovenproof dish and spread with a thin layer of ricotta mixture. Repeat layering with remaining vegetables, spreading the ricotta mixture between each layer and finishing with ricotta mixture on top.

combine extra parmesan with breadcrumbs and sprinkle on top. Drizzle over extra oil.

bake gratin for 35–40 minutes. Place under the grill to brown for a few minutes if necessary. Rest gratin for 20 minutes before serving.

serving suggestions
Serve with a side of salad greens with black olives and drizzle with olive oil and balsamic vinegar.

SAVOURY SECRETS
GF breadcrumbs* see **cook's tips — bread** (page 210).

Vegetables can be baked or grilled on the barbecue. They can be prepared 2 days in advance.

You can substitute pecorino or Romano cheese for the parmesan.

This gratin will keep well for 2 days.

millet pilaff with saffron & green vegetables

Millet is a highly nutritious cereal grain with a delicious nutty taste. It is, of course, gluten-free and easy to digest.

SERVES 4

millet pilaff

20 g (¾ oz) unsalted butter

1 tablespoon olive oil (you may require a little more)

1 onion or leek, white part only, rinsed well, finely chopped

1 celery stalk, finely chopped

2 garlic cloves, crushed

2–3 makrut (kaffir lime) leaves

zest of 1 large lemon, finely grated, and reserve 2½ tablespoons juice

315 g (11¼ oz/1½ cups) hulled millet

125 ml (4 fl oz/½ cup) dry white wine

1 litre (35 fl oz/4 cups) hot **GF** vegetable or **GF** chicken stock (for non-vegetarian)

¼ teaspoon saffron threads

35 g (1¼ oz/¼ cup) currants

additional ingredients

1 bunch asparagus, trimmed and cut into 6 cm (2½ inch) lengths

1 bunch broccolini, cut into 5 cm (2 inch) lengths

125 g (4½ oz) snow peas (mangetout) or sugar snap peas

80 g (2¾ oz/½ cup) blanched almonds, toasted

heat butter and oil in a large frying pan (with a fitted lid) or use a risotto pan over medium–high heat. Add onion and celery and sauté until softened. Add garlic, makrut leaves and zest and cook briefly.

add millet and stir until it is well coated with butter and oil mixture. Cook for 2 minutes, moving the millet around the pan. Add wine and bring to the boil. It will evaporate quickly.

add stock and saffron threads. Season with salt and freshly ground black pepper. Bring to the boil then reduce the heat immediately to low. Cover with lid and simmer gently, undisturbed, for 15 minutes. The millet will absorb all of the stock. At the end of cooking time, add lemon juice and currants. Stir the pilaff gently with a fork. Cover again and leave to rest for 10 minutes.

prepare vegetables and steam or blanch while pilaff is resting.

serve pilaff with steamed vegetables and almonds.

SAVOURY SECRETS

Millet pilaff is a good substitute for couscous.

To vary the recipe, prepare millet pilaff as above, adding 1 teaspoon sumac* after the onion. Add small pieces of roasted pumpkin (winter squash), coriander (cilantro) leaves and toasted pine nuts to finish. Serve hot or cold as a salad.

Sumac* is a Lebanese lemon-scented spice with a rich earthy colour. It goes well with fish, squid, chicken and lamb, sprinkled over hummus or in pilaff.

pasta with smoky sweet potato & ricotta

This pasta dish has a distinctive smoky flavour as it contains both sweet smoked paprika and smoked cheese.

SERVES 4

1 tablespoon olive oil

20 g (¾ oz) unsalted butter, melted

1 garlic clove, crushed

1 teaspoon sweet smoked paprika

600 g (1 lb 5 oz) sweet potato, peeled and cut into 2.5 cm (1 inch) chunks

3 tablespoons blanched almonds

450 g (1 lb) **GF** penne or **GF** pasta shells

125 ml (4 fl oz/½ cup) pouring (whipping) cream

125 ml (4 fl oz/½ cup) well-flavoured **GF** vegetable or **GF** chicken stock (for non-vegetarian)

2 tablespoons lemon thyme leaves, plus extra leaves, to serve

125 g (4½ oz) **GF** smoked cheese, grated

250 g (9 oz/1 cup) ricotta cheese, drained in a paper towel-lined colander

line a baking tray with baking paper.

preheat oven to 200°C (400°F/Gas 6).

combine oil, butter, garlic and paprika in a large mixing bowl. Season with salt and freshly ground black pepper. Add sweet potato and toss to coat.

place sweet potato on a baking tray and bake for 25–30 minutes or until tender. Add the almonds to the mixing bowl, coating in the remaining oil mixture. You can add the almonds to the baking for the last 5 minutes of cooking time but be sure to keep an eye on them as they brown quickly.

cook pasta in a large saucepan in plenty of boiling salted water until *al dente*. Drain pasta and return it to the saucepan. Cover and set aside briefly.

place cream, stock and thyme in a small saucepan over high heat and bring to the boil. Reduce heat to medium and cook for several minutes until reduced slightly. Remove from heat and add smoked cheese. Season with salt and freshly ground black pepper. Stir until cheese melts. Pour sauce over pasta, stirring gently to combine.

divide between heated bowls, top with sweet potato and a good dollop of ricotta. Sprinkle with almonds and extra thyme leaves.

SAVOURY SECRETS
Substitute pumpkin (winter squash) for the sweet potato.
Add grilled or pan-fried **GF** pancetta or **GF** chorizo sausage for a non-vegetarian pasta dish.
Baby English spinach leaves can be incorporated as soon as the pasta is cooked or served with the pasta.

red capsicum & lentil potpies with feta crumble

The crumble topping adds both texture and flavour to the potpies. They are very nice eaten cold and are good picnic fare.

SERVES 4

feta crumble

110 g (3¾ oz/1 cup) **GF** breadcrumbs*

1 tablespoon chopped flat-leaf (Italian) parsley

2 rosemary sprigs, finely chopped

75 g (2¾ oz/½ cup) crumbled Greek feta cheese

40 g (1½ oz) unsalted butter, melted

potpies

20 g (¾ oz) unsalted butter

1 red onion, finely chopped

1 large red capsicum (pepper), seeded, membrane removed and cut into 1 cm (½ inch) slices

1 garlic clove, crushed

½ quantity prepared **lentils du puy** (page 109)

75 g (2¾ oz/½ cup) crumbled Greek feta cheese

2 tablespoons roughly chopped flat-leaf (Italian) parsley

3 x 60 g (2¼ oz) eggs

60 ml (2 fl oz/¼ cup) pouring (whipping) cream

line four 250 ml (9 fl oz/1 cup) capacity pie tins or ceramic pots with baking paper measuring 20 x 20 cm (8 x 8 inches). This makes it easy to remove the pies from the tins and keeps the crumble in place.

preheat oven to 180°C (350°F/Gas 4).

combine feta crumble ingredients in a bowl, mix well and reserve.

place butter in a frying pan and sauté onion and capsicum over medium–low heat for about 5 minutes until soft. Add garlic and sauté briefly. Remove from heat and stir in the lentils, feta and parsley.

spoon lentil mixture into lined pie tins and place on a baking tray.

whisk eggs and cream together and pour over lentil mixture. Top potpies with feta crumble.

bake for 25–30 minutes until set and crumble is golden. Test with a skewer. If egg mixture is set, the skewer will come out clean.

serving suggestions
Prepare a salad with rocket, grilled eggplant (aubergine) and/or **slow-roasted tomatoes** (page 168) and black olives. Dress with olive oil and red wine vinegar or vin cotto**.

SAVOURY SECRETS
You can make eight smaller potpies in a muffin tray lined with baking paper. Bake for about 20 minutes.

GF breadcrumbs* see **cook's tips — bread** (page 210).

Vin cotto** is an Italian wine vinegar that is available in speciality stores.

SIDE DISHES

salads

salsas

vegetables

apple, mint & ruby grapefruit salad

This is a delightfully refreshing salad. It goes well with fish, chicken and pork.

SERVES 4

2 ruby red grapefruit

125 g (4½ oz) mixed green salad leaves including watercress, leaves picked from the stalks

1 sweet apple, such as lady william or red delicious, thinly sliced (see note)

1 tablespoon small mint or basil leaves

70 g (2½ oz/½ cup) unsalted pistachio nuts

grapefruit dressing

2 teaspoons red wine vinegar

1 teaspoon **GF** dijon mustard

1 tablespoon grapefruit juice, squeezed from two reserved rounds*

1 garlic clove, crushed

½ teaspoon sugar or honey

2½ tablespoons olive oil

place grapefruit on a chopping board and use a sharp knife to cut a slice from each end. Cut away the peel working from top to bottom, removing the white pith with the peel. Cut grapefruit into rounds, reserving two for the dressing*.

whisk dressing ingredients together in a small bowl and set aside. Thin dressing with a little water if necessary.

place green salad leaves in a bowl or on a platter. Arrange grapefruit, apple and mint over the top and sprinkle with pistachios. Pour dressing over to serve.

note: Prepare the apple just before serving the salad or squeeze a little lemon juice over to prevent browning.

SAVOURY SECRETS
Substitute blood oranges for the ruby red grapefruit.
Substitute avocado for the apple. Prepare the avocado just before serving the salad.

asian greens & cucumber salad

This salad is simple and delicious. Serve it with fish, chicken, beef or pork.

SERVES 4

chilli lime dressing

1 long red chilli, seeded and finely chopped, to taste

1 garlic clove, crushed

1 teaspoon grated fresh ginger

1 tablespoon grated light palm sugar (jaggery)* or 1 teaspoon soft brown sugar

2 teaspoons **GF** fish sauce

1 tablespoon lime juice

1½ tablespoons vegetable or grape seed oil

½ teaspoon sesame oil

salad

2 cups Asian salad greens**

10 g (¼ oz/⅓ cup) combined coriander (cilantro) leaves and mint leaves

1 Lebanese (short) cucumber, peeled, seeded and thinly sliced

2–3 spring onions (scallions), thinly sliced on an angle

3 small red radishes, very thinly sliced (optional)

whisk dressing ingredients together in a small bowl and set aside.

combine salad ingredients in a bowl. Pour dressing over to serve.

SAVOURY SECRETS

To vary the recipe, add bean sprouts to the salad.

If it is hardened, microwave palm sugar* for a few seconds on medium heat as this will make grating easier.

Grow your own Asian salad greens**. You can often buy a punnet of seedlings with four varieties including mild Tah Tsai (Tatsoi), peppery red mustard and Japanese greens Mizuna and Mibuna. You simply cut as many leaves as required for your salad.

avocado, pear & parmesan salad

The flavours and textures of crisp and creamy ingredients make this salad very delicious.

SERVES 4–6

walnut oil dressing

1 tablespoon verjuice or white wine vinegar

1 teaspoon lemon juice

½ garlic clove, crushed

½ teaspoon sugar

1 teaspoon **GF** dijon mustard

1 spring onion (scallion), very finely chopped

2½ tablespoons walnut oil

1 tablespoon grape seed oil

salad

60 g (2¼ oz/½ cup) walnuts

1 lemon, juice only

1–2 avocados (depending on size), sliced

2 or 3 small just-ripe pears, cored and cut
into eight wedges

70 g (2½ oz) salad leaves, such as baby cos
(romaine) lettuce, rocket (arugula) or
baby English spinach, rinsed well and drained

shaved parmesan cheese, to finish

preheat oven to 180°C (350°F/Gas 4).

whisk walnut oil dressing ingredients together with salt and freshly ground black pepper in a small bowl and set aside.

place walnuts on a baking tray and roast for 10 minutes. Wrap immediately in a clean tea towel (dish towel) and rub to peel off skins. Reserve walnuts and discard skins. Cool walnuts.

squeeze lemon juice over the avocado slices and pear wedges.

place salad leaves in a bowl or on a platter, arrange avocado, pear and parmesan on top. Drizzle with dressing and sprinkle with walnuts.

SAVOURY SECRETS
Substitute pecan or toasted pine nuts for the walnuts.
Substitute crumbly feta for the parmesan.

baby spinach & mango salad with lime drizzle

This salad is the perfect match to have with **spicy chicken** (page 98), and also goes very well with fish and prawns.

SERVES 4

lime drizzle

60 g (2¼ oz/¼ cup) **GF** whole-egg mayonnaise*

80 g (2¾ oz/⅓ cup) **GF** Greek-style yoghurt

zest of 1 lime, finely grated and reserved juice

1 teaspoon **GF** dijon mustard

salad

85 g (3 oz) baby English spinach leaves

1–2 firm ripe mangoes, peeled and sliced into ribbons using a vegetable peeler

1 Lebanese (short) cucumber, peeled and sliced into ribbons using a vegetable peeler

1 small red onion, thinly sliced

15 g (½ oz/½ cup) coriander (cilantro) leaves (optional)

whisk lime drizzle ingredients together in a small bowl. Add a little water to thin the dressing if necessary. Transfer to a jug and set aside.

place spinach leaves, mango, cucumber, onion and coriander, if using, on a platter or individual plates. Pour lime drizzle over to serve.

SAVOURY SECRETS

GF whole-egg mayonnaise* is available from supermarkets. Alternatively, prepare **whole-egg mayonnaise** (page 201).

This salad is especially good for a crowd as it can be prepared in advance.

To vary the salad, sprinkle pine nuts or macadamia nuts over to serve.

baked beetroot, feta & pistachio salad

This salad can be made several hours in advance and dressed just before serving. Place in the refrigerator until required.

dressing

zest of 1 orange, finely grated and reserved juice

2 tablespoons olive oil

1 garlic clove, crushed

1 teaspoon tarragon vinegar

drizzle of honey, to taste (optional)

salad

2 bunches baby beetroot (beets) or 4 medium-sized beetroot, trimmed and rinsed well

1½ tablespoons olive oil

juice of 1 orange

70 g (2½ oz/2 cups) rocket (arugula)

6 radicchio leaves, torn into pieces

30 green beans, trimmed and cooked in boiling water for 3–4 minutes until just tender

150 g (5½ oz/1 cup) feta cheese, broken into small pieces

50 g (1¾ oz/⅓ cup) unsalted pistachio nuts

preheat oven to 180°C (350°F/Gas 4).

whisk dressing ingredients with freshly ground black pepper together in a small bowl and set aside.

place beetroot on one or two sheets of foil. Drizzle with ½ tablespoon olive oil and wrap securely in the foil. Place on a baking tray and bake for about 45 minutes or until tender when pierced with a skewer. Cool beetroot a little. Wearing latex gloves to avoid staining your hands, peel skins and discard. If using medium–sized beetroot, cut into quarters.

combine orange juice with remaining olive oil and pour over warm beetroot, allow to marinate for 1 hour or more.

place rocket and radicchio leaves on a platter. Remove beetroot from marinade and discard marinade. Place beans, beetroot and feta over leaves and sprinkle with pistachios. Pour dressing over to serve.

SAVOURY SECRET

To vary the recipe, add roasted red onions. Cut onions in quarters leaving the skin on. Brush onions with olive oil, place on a baking tray and bake in the oven with the beetroot. Remove skin when onions are cooked.

blood orange, fennel & olive salad

This is a very versatile salad as it goes with poultry, fish, prawns or lamb. I sometimes like to serve it on a platter rather than in a bowl.

SERVES 4–6

2 blood oranges

2 small fennel bulbs, shaved

70 g (2½ oz/2 cups) rocket (arugula), or other salad leaves

24 kalamata olives

citrus vinaigrette

1 garlic clove, crushed

1 tablespoon white wine vinegar (or verjuice)

1 tablespoon fresh orange juice

1 teaspoon lime or lemon juice

1 teaspoon **GF** dijon mustard

½ teaspoon sugar or honey

80 ml (2½ fl oz/⅓ cup) olive oil (or use half olive oil and half grape seed oil)

place oranges on a chopping board. With a sharp knife cut away the peel, working from top to bottom removing the pith with the peel. Cut oranges between the membranes into segments.

whisk vinaigrette ingredients with salt and freshly ground black pepper together in a small bowl and set aside. Thin with a little water if necessary.

combine salad ingredients and drizzle with citrus vinaigrette to serve.

SAVOURY SECRETS
Substitute other varieties of oranges for the blood oranges.

To shave fennel, use a mandolin or vegetable peeler.

To curl and crisp fennel, place shaved fennel in a bowl of iced water. Leave to soak for about 30 minutes until fennel curls and becomes crisp. Drain and pat dry with paper towel or spin in a salad spinner to remove water.

cannellini bean & chorizo salad

I always have tinned beans of every variety in my pantry. They are so versatile as they can be eaten warm or cold. With the addition of a few simple ingredients, you can have a meal ready in minutes. This salad is delicious with grilled lamb or chicken and is perfect to take on a picnic.

SERVES 4

1 **GF** chorizo sausage, thinly sliced

400 g (14 oz) tin cannellini beans, drained and rinsed

1 green capsicum (pepper), seeded, membrane removed and diced

1 small red onion, thinly sliced

3 tomatoes, cut into thin wedges

2 tablespoons capers, rinsed well if salted and drained on paper towel

24 mixed marinated olives, such as chilli olives

2 teaspoons finely chopped rosemary

10 g (¼ oz/½ cup) flat-leaf (Italian) parsley leaves, plus extra leaves, to finish

dressing

oil from frying chorizo

1 garlic clove, crushed

2 tablespoons olive oil

zest of 1 lemon, finely grated

2 teaspoons red wine vinegar

heat a frying pan over medium heat and cook chorizo until lightly browned. Using a slotted spoon, remove chorizo from pan and drain on paper towel. Set aside. Reserve oil in pan.

add garlic and olive oil to chorizo oil remaining in the pan and cook briefly. Turn off the heat then add lemon zest and vinegar. Season with freshly ground black pepper. Stir well to combine.

place chorizo and remaining salad ingredients in a bowl and gently combine.

pour warm dressing over salad to serve.

SAVOURY SECRET
Vary the herbs with whatever you have on hand. Fresh mint and coriander (cilantro) work well.

roasted vegetable salad

This salad is delicious served warm or cold and is great to take on a picnic.

SERVES 4

60 ml (2 fl oz/¼ cup) olive oil

1 garlic clove, crushed

400 g (14 oz) butternut pumpkin (squash), peeled and cut into 2.5 cm (1 inch) chunks

2 medium fennel bulbs or celeriac, trimmed and cut into quarters

2 red onions, cut into quarters (leave the outer skin attached and remove after baking)

2 zucchini (courgettes), cut on an angle in 2.5 cm (1 inch) pieces

basil leaves, to finish

olive oil, extra, to drizzle

pomegranate molasses* or balsamic vinegar, to finish

line two baking trays with baking paper.

preheat oven to 180°C (350°F/Gas 4).

combine oil and garlic in a large bowl. Add the prepared vegetables and toss to coat. Place on baking trays and season to taste with salt and freshly ground black pepper. Bake for 25 minutes. Remove any cooked vegetables. Turn remaining vegetables and cook for a further 15 minutes or until tender.

place the roasted vegetables on a serving platter and scatter the basil leaves over them. Drizzle salad with extra olive oil and pomegranate molasses just before serving.

SAVOURY SECRETS

Pomegranate molasses* is made from pomegranate juice, sugar and lemon juice. It is a piquant syrupy liquid and is available at speciality gourmet stores or Middle Eastern grocery stores.

Salad may be prepared and refrigerated several hours in advance.

To vary the recipe, add pieces of eggplant (aubergine) to the vegetables and bake as above.

You can also add crumbled feta to the salad and sprinkle with toasted pine nuts to serve.

tomatoes with pomegranate drizzle

Choose tomatoes that are ripe and full of flavour as they star in this salad. The pomegranate drizzle adds a wonderful sweet-sour taste that complements the tomatoes.

SERVES 4

6 tomatoes, sliced

10 g (¼ oz/½ cup) small mint or basil leaves, rinsed and gently patted dry with paper towel

toasted pine nuts, to finish (optional)

pomegranate drizzle

1 tablespoon raspberry vinegar

2 teaspoons pomegranate molasses*

1 teaspoon lemon juice

1 small garlic clove, crushed

80 ml (2½ fl oz/⅓ cup) olive oil

2 teaspoons chopped mint or basil

whisk drizzle ingredients with freshly ground black pepper together in a small bowl and set aside.

arrange tomatoes on a platter, scatter over mint leaves and pine nuts, if using. Dress with pomegranate drizzle to serve.

SAVOURY SECRETS

Pomegranate molasses* is made from pomegranate juice, sugar and lemon juice. It is a piquant syrupy liquid and is available at speciality gourmet stores and Middle Eastern grocery stores.

Use pomegranate molasses in salad dressings, glazes and marinades for chicken, quail, pork or lamb.

Substitute fresh figs for the tomatoes.

To vary the recipe, tear two large buffalo mozzarella in pieces and serve with tomatoes or figs, rocket (arugula), pine nuts and pomegranate drizzle. This makes a delightful summer starter or salad.

guacamole salsa

I love tasting and identifying the ingredients in this salsa, unlike a puréed guacamole.

hot & spicy corn & avocado salsa

This salsa goes well with barbecued fish, chicken, pork or grilled beef. I like it spooned over shredded chicken and sour cream and wrapped in a soft white corn tortilla.

SERVES 4

2 large firm avocados, diced

3 tomatoes, cored, seeded and diced

1 celery stalk, finely diced

2 spring onions (scallions), thinly sliced

1 long red or green chilli, seeded and very finely chopped, to taste

7 g (⅛ oz/¼ cup) coriander (cilantro) leaves

zest i 1–2 limes, finely grated and reserved juice

1–2 garlic cloves, crushed

olive oil, to drizzle

preserved sliced jalapeño peppers*, to finish (optional)

combine avocado, tomato, celery, spring onion, chilli and coriander in a large bowl.

combine lime zest and juice and garlic in a small bowl. Pour over salsa. Drizzle generously with olive oil and top with jalapeño peppers, if using, to serve.

serving suggestions
Serve salsa with **chilli beef** (page 102), fish or chicken. It's also great with anything wrapped in a soft white corn tortilla.

SAVOURY SECRET
Preserved sliced jalapeño peppers* are available in jars in the supermarket.

SERVES 4

2 corn cobs

1 small red capsicum (pepper), seeded, membrane removed and diced

3 spring onions (scallions), thinly sliced

1 avocado, diced

7 g (⅛ oz/¼ cup) coriander (cilantro) leaves, or a combination of coriander and mint

dressing

1 red or green chilli, seeded and finely chopped, to taste

1 garlic clove, crushed

2 tablespoons olive oil

zest of 1 lime, finely grated and reserve 1 tablespoon juice

1 teaspoon runny honey

½ teaspoon ground cumin

whisk dressing ingredients together in a small bowl and set aside.

hold a cob of corn upright on a chopping board. Use a large sharp knife and cut downwards from the top, as close to the core as possible, to remove the kernels.

blanch corn kernels in boiling water for 30 seconds or until tender. Drain and refresh under cold water.

combine corn with remaining salsa ingredients in a bowl. Pour dressing over salsa to serve.

SAVOURY SECRET
To vary the recipe, lightly brush corn cobs with oil and barbecue for about 15 minutes on medium heat until lightly charred on all sides. Cut corn kernels from the cob and add to salsa.

preserved lemon & caper salsa

This punchy salsa works well with pan-fried or grilled fish, prawns, chicken or lamb.

SERVES 4

1 tablespoon capers, rinsed well if salted and drained on paper towel

2 spring onions (scallions), thinly sliced, or use 6 chives

1 celery stalk, finely diced

2 pieces preserved lemon*, pulp discarded, rind rinsed and thinly sliced

½ Lebanese (small) cucumber, peeled, seeded and finely diced

12 black olives, pitted and thinly sliced (optional)

1 tablespoon thinly sliced flat-leaf (Italian) parsley

2 teaspoons dry sherry

1 tablespoon lime juice

1 tablespoon olive oil

place all ingredients in a bowl and gently stir to combine.

SAVOURY SECRET
Preserved lemons* are available in supermarkets or prepare **preserved lemons** (page 202).

sweet & spicy mango salsa

Serve this salsa with fish, prawns or chicken.

SERVES 4–6

1 small red onion, finely chopped

1 small red capsicum (pepper), seeded, membrane removed, cut into 1 cm (½ inch) dice, or use 1 tomato, diced

1 firm mango, peeled and cut into 1 cm (½ inch) dice

2 teaspoons grated fresh ginger

1 red or green chilli, seeded and finely chopped, to taste

1 garlic clove, crushed

2 teaspoons sesame oil

2 teaspoons olive oil

juice of 1 lime

1 tablespoon shredded mint

place all ingredients in a bowl and gently stir to combine.

SAVOURY SECRET
Substitute papaya for the mango.

baked pumpkin with sweet smoked paprika

This baked pumpkin has a sweet smoky flavour and tastes absolutely delicious.

SERVES 6

500 g (1 lb 2 oz) butternut pumpkin (squash), peeled and cut into 2.5 cm (1 inch) chunks

1 tablespoon olive oil

20 g (¾ oz) butter, melted

sweet smoked paprika

line a baking tray with baking paper.

preheat oven to 180°C (350°F/Gas 4).

place pumpkin in a large bowl, add oil and butter and toss to coat.

transfer pumpkin to the baking tray and sprinkle all sides with paprika. Season with salt and freshly ground black pepper.

bake for about 30–35 minutes or until golden and tender.

SAVOURY SECRET
Substitute sweet potato for the pumpkin.

creamy fennel & potato gratin

SERVES 4

250 ml (9 fl oz/1 cup) milk

250 ml (9 fl oz/1 cup) thickened (whipping) cream

1 garlic clove, crushed

2 bay leaves

500 g (1 lb 2 oz) fennel bulbs (approximately 1 large or 2 small bulbs), very thinly sliced

500 g (1 lb 2 oz) desiree potatoes, very thinly sliced

65 g (2½ oz/½ cup) grated gruyère or cheddar cheese

50 g (1¾ oz) gruyère cheese, extra, grated

50 g (1¾ oz) **GF** breadcrumbs*

15 g (½ oz) unsalted butter

freshly grated nutmeg, to finish

grease a gratin dish or a 24 x 24 cm x 5 cm (9½ x 9½ x 2 inch) square ovenproof dish and line base with baking paper.

preheat oven to 180°C (350°F/Gas 4).

place milk, cream, garlic and bay leaves in a saucepan over medium–high heat and bring to the boil. Turn heat off. Season with salt and freshly ground black pepper and leave to infuse.

combine fennel, potato and cheese in a large bowl and transfer to prepared ovenproof dish.

remove bay leaves from the infused liquid and pour over the fennel and potato mixture.

combine extra gruyère cheese and breadcrumbs and sprinkle over the top. Dot gratin with butter and dust with grated nutmeg.

bake for 1 hour or until cooked. If gratin is browning too much, cover dish loosely with foil. Potatoes should be soft and will absorb the liquid. Allow gratin to stand for 10 minutes before serving.

serving suggestion
This creamy combination of vegetables is perfect served with roasts or alongside a succulent steak topped with **caramelised shallot sauce** (page 199).

SAVOURY SECRETS
Use a mandolin or food processor fitted with a slicing blade to finely slice the fennel and potatoes.

GF breadcrumbs* see **cook's tips — bread** (page 210).

Substitute celeriac for the fennel. Celeriac has a wonderful earthy flavour and goes perfectly with potatoes in a gratin.

crisp parsnip ribbons or 'spaghetti'

Parsnips are such a versatile vegetable. They can be baked, glazed, mashed and sliced into ribbons or julienne and fried until crisp and golden.

SERVES 4

2–3 parsnips

vegetable or bran oil for frying (see note).

sea salt, to serve

peel parsnips, then, using a vegetable peeler, slice into thin ribbons. Alternatively, use a julienne peeler to make 'spaghetti'. Do not use the bitter woody centre of the parsnip.

heat oil in a frying pan or saucepan and when hot (but not smoking), fry just one parsnip ribbon or 'spaghetti' strand to test the heat of the oil. If it is too hot and the parsnip blackens, remove oil from heat briefly and wait for it to cool down a little. When the oil is ready, fry a small amount of parsnip ribbons, move them gently around in the oil using tongs. They will take a minute or so to turn pale golden. Do not brown too much.

remove to paper towel to drain. Repeat with remaining parsnip ribbons or spaghetti strands. Sprinkle with sea salt to serve.

note: The quantity of oil will depend on the size of your frying pan/saucepan, but as a guide pour in 3–4 centimetres (1¼–1½ inches).

SAVOURY SECRETS
Parsnip ribbons or 'spaghetti' can be prepared up to 2 hours in advance. Once fried and after draining on paper towel, place on foil so that they do not soften before serving. Do not reheat. Serve as a vegetable or garnish with puréed potato and/or parsnip or with soup.

green beans with hazelnut oil & roasted hazelnuts

SERVES 4

70 g (2½ oz/½ cup) hazelnuts*

4 handfuls whole green beans, trimmed

2–3 teaspoons hazelnut oil

sea salt, to serve

preheat oven to 180°C (350°F/Gas 4).

place hazelnuts on a baking tray and roast for about 10 minutes until the skins darken. Wrap nuts in a clean tea towel (dish towel) and rub to remove skins. Discard skins. Roughly chop nuts and reserve.

steam or cook beans uncovered in a saucepan of boiling salted water over high heat for 4–5 minutes until just tender. Drain beans, pat dry with paper towel and reserve.

add hazelnut oil to the saucepan and warm briefly then add reserved beans. Season with salt. Turn beans over with tongs to coat with the oil.

place beans on a warm platter and top with hazelnuts. Sprinkle with sea salt to serve.

SAVOURY SECRET
You can purchase hazelnuts* already roasted if you wish.

harissa potatoes

I love these potatoes as they absorb the flavours of the stock and harissa. They go well with rosemary and garlic studded lamb, marinated sirloin beef or grilled chicken with lemon and herbs. They are also great for serving a larger number of guests when entertaining.

SERVES 6

6 large all-purpose potatoes, such as desiree or sebago, peeled and cut into large chunks

1 large or 2 medium-sized red onions, cut into eight wedges

500 ml (17 fl oz/2 cups) **GF** chicken stock

1 tablespoon **GF** tomato paste (concentrated purée)

1 teaspoon harissa paste*, or to taste

sweet smoked paprika

olive oil, for drizzling

roasted red capsicum (page 164) (optional), cut into long strips

grated parmesan cheese (optional)

lightly grease an ovenproof dish, one that will hold the potatoes and onions fairly close together in a single layer.

preheat oven to 180°C (350°F/Gas 4).

place potato and onion in the ovenproof dish.

combine stock, tomato paste and harissa in a jug. Season with freshly ground black pepper and pour over potato and onion. Sprinkle with paprika and drizzle lightly with oil.

bake for 1–1½ hours until potato is cooked and most of the liquid has been absorbed.

remove from oven and place capsicum, if using, here and there over potato and onion and/or sprinkle with parmesan. Bake for another 15 minutes.

SAVOURY SECRET
Harissa paste* is a traditional accompaniment to Tunisian dishes. It is a wonderful, vibrant red, hot paste made with chilli. It is available in supermarkets and speciality stores.

lemon & parsley potatoes

These potatoes are particularly delicious served with fish. Use new, coliban, desiree, pontiac or sebago potatoes.

SERVES 4

4–6 medium–large all-purpose potatoes, peeled and cut into 2.5 cm (1 inch) pieces

15 g (½ oz) unsalted butter, melted

3 teaspoons olive oil

2 tablespoons finely chopped flat-leaf (Italian) parsley

zest of 1–2 lemons, finely grated

line a baking tray with baking paper.

preheat oven to 180°C (350°F/Gas 4).

parboil potato in a large saucepan of boiling, salted water over high heat for 3 minutes. Drain and pat dry with paper towel.

combine butter and oil and brush over potato pieces. Season with salt and freshly ground black pepper. Place on the baking tray and bake for 20 minutes.

combine parsley and lemon zest. Sprinkle over potato and bake for a further 15 minutes or until potato is golden and tender.

red onion & fennel confit

This confit is superb with grilled steak, barbecued lamb chops or roast lamb. It is a great accompaniment to cold meats and is especially good with ham in a toasted sandwich. It will keep in the refrigerator for up to a week and can be served warm or cold.

MAKES 1 CUP

20 g (¾ oz) unsalted butter

2 teaspoons olive oil

1 teaspoon fennel seeds

150 g (5½ oz) red onion, thinly sliced

150 g (5½ oz) fennel bulb, thinly sliced

1 garlic clove, crushed

80 ml (2½ fl oz/⅓ cup) balsamic vinegar

2 tablespoons soft brown sugar, firmly packed

1 long red chilli, seeded and finely chopped, to taste (optional)

heat butter and oil in a heavy-based frying pan over low–medium heat. Add fennel seeds and onion and cook for about 7 minutes or until onion is softened.

add fennel and cook, stirring occasionally, for 3 minutes.

add garlic and cook briefly, then add vinegar, sugar and chilli, if using. Simmer for about 20 minutes or until vegetables soften and liquid becomes syrupy.

roasted red capsicum

These roasted red capsicums are a favourite of mine as they are so versatile. I use them in many recipes including dips, soups, sauces, side vegetables and salads.

SERVES 8

2 kg (4 lb 8 oz) red capsicums (peppers), rinsed and patted dry with paper towel

line a baking tray with baking paper.

preheat oven to 200°C (400°F/Gas 6).

place capsicums on the baking tray and bake for 30–35 minutes until skins blister and blacken.

transfer capsicum to a deep bowl. Cover with plastic wrap and cool.

remove capsicum from bowl, peel and discard skins, membranes and seeds. Cut in halves or strips.

SAVOURY SECRETS

Strain and reserve any liquid from the roasted capsicum as it is delicious added to salad dressings, sauces or soups. The liquid can be frozen.

Serve roasted red capsicum as part of an antipasto platter or warm in the microwave as a side vegetable topped with feta cheese and olives.

To freeze roasted red capsicum see **cook's tips — capsicum (peppers)** (page 210).

roughed-up roasted potatoes

I really could live on potatoes — it must be the Irish in me! Use coliban, desiree, pontiac or sebago potatoes.

6–8 large all-purpose potatoes, peeled and cut into large even-sized pieces

125 ml (4 fl oz/½ cup) olive oil

1 tablespoon chopped herbs, such as thyme and rosemary (optional)

1 garlic clove, crushed

zest of 1–2 lemons, finely grated, or 2 pieces preserved lemon, pulp discarded, rind rinsed and finely chopped

line a baking tray with baking paper.

preheat oven to 200°C (400°F/Gas 6).

parboil potato in boiling salted water over high heat. Drain well and pat dry with paper towel. When potatoes are cool enough to handle, use a fork to roughen the surface.

combine oil, herbs, if using, garlic and lemon zest.

dip potatoes into oil mixture and then place on the baking tray. Season with salt and freshly ground black pepper.

bake for 45 minutes or until potatoes are tender, crispy and golden.

slow-roasted tomatoes

The rich intensity of these tomatoes is superb.

SERVING SIZE

2 kg (4 lb 8 oz) ripe roma (plum) or vine-ripened tomatoes, cut in half and core removed

1–2 garlic cloves, crushed

60 ml (2 fl oz/¼ cup) olive oil

2 tablespoons finely chopped rosemary

line two baking trays with baking paper.

preheat oven to 170°C (325°F/Gas 3).

place cut tomatoes in a large bowl.

whisk remaining ingredients together with salt and freshly ground black pepper, to taste, and drizzle over tomatoes. Use your hands to turn the tomatoes to coat.

place tomatoes cut side up on the baking trays.

bake for 30 minutes then reduce oven temperature to 120°C (235°F/Gas ½) and bake for a further 45 minutes.

note: The longer and slower you cook the tomatoes, the more the flavour will develop and intensify. If you have time, you can cook the tomatoes at a lower temperature for a longer period of time.

SAVOURY SECRETS

Slow-roasted tomatoes will keep for 3 days in the refrigerator. They also freeze well.

Substitute other herbs for rosemary, for example parsley, basil, oregano or thyme. Dried herbs work well too. You can also omit the herbs and drizzle the tomatoes with balsamic vinegar before baking.

Serve as part of an antipasto platter.

Spread on **GF** toast or canapé and top with soft goat's curd and basil.

Use in salads, especially with mozzarella, kalamata olives, basil and a drizzle of olive oil.

SWEET FOOD

cupcakes, butterfly cakes & fairy cakes

Who does not love a cupcake? Whether for a children's party, afternoon tea or simply a treat for your family, you are probably going to make these little cakes again and again. They keep well for two days. Undecorated cakes may be frozen.

MAKES 10 CUPCAKES OR
20 MINI CAKES

cupcakes

100 g (3½ oz) unsalted butter, softened

110 g (3¾ oz/½ cup) caster (superfine) sugar

½ teaspoon vanilla bean paste or natural vanilla extract

2 x 60 g (2¼ oz) eggs

75 g (2¾ oz/½ cup) GF self-raising flour*

30 g (1 oz/¼ cup) pure maize cornflour (cornstarch)

60 g (2¼ oz/⅓ cup) white rice flour

1 teaspoon GF baking powder

½ teaspoon bicarbonate of soda (baking soda)

90 g (3¼ oz/⅓ cup) GF Greek-style yoghurt

2 tablespoons milk (approximately)

frosting

50 g (1¾ oz) unsalted butter, softened

50 g (1¾ oz) cream cheese, at room temperature, cut into cubes

185 g (6½ oz/1½ cups) pure icing (confectioners') sugar, sifted if lumpy

1 teaspoon lemon juice

¼ teaspoon vanilla bean paste or natural vanilla extract

GF food colouring and GF decorations

insert paper (patty pan) cases into muffin tray/s. Fill any empty muffin holes with water so that the cakes bake evenly.

preheat oven to 180°C (350°F/Gas 4).

for the cupcakes

cream butter, sugar and vanilla in the small bowl of an electric mixer until light and fluffy. Add eggs one at a time, beating well after each addition. Scrape down side of bowl.

sift flours, baking powder and bicarbonate of soda together and fold into creamed mixture, alternately with the yoghurt. Scrape down the sides of bowl. Stir in milk a little at a time to achieve a soft batter consistency. Fill each paper case about three-quarters full, then bake for 25 minutes or until lightly golden and cooked through. Test with a skewer. Mini cakes will take about 12 minutes to cook.

cool for 5 minutes before removing to a wire rack and cool completely before icing and decorating.

for the frosting

place butter, cream cheese, icing sugar, lemon juice and vanilla in a food processor and blend well. Add food colouring a drop at a time. The frosting can be made while the cakes are baking.

SWEET SECRETS

GF self-raising flour* —I use either F.G. Roberts gluten-free self-raising flour **or** Orgran gluten-free self-raising flour. They are available in some supermarkets and health food stores.

To make **butterfly cakes** bake cupcake recipe as above. Use a fine-pointed knife to cut circles 1 cm (½ inch) in from the edge and about 1 cm (½ inch) down into the cakes. Fill the hole with jam and cream. Cut the cut-out circles of cake in half and position them on top of the cream so they look like butterfly wings. Place jam between the wings for the butterfly's body. Dust with icing sugar.

To make **fairy cakes** bake cupcake recipe as above. Use a fine pointed knife to cut circles 1 cm (½ inch) in from the edge and about 1.5 cm (⅝ inch) down into the cakes. Fill the hole with jam or lemon butter and pipe a swirl of sweetened cream on top. Place cut-out cake circles on top of the cream. Dust with pure icing sugar.

dark chocolate budino with cheat's honeycomb ice cream

Budino means pudding in Italian. These puddings are delectably rich and ever so simple to prepare. They can be made well in advance too.

SERVES 5 OR 6

cheat's honeycomb ice cream

1 litre **GF** vanilla ice cream*, softened

100 g (3½ oz) **GF** honeycomb**, crushed, reserve a little to place on top of ice-cream balls to serve

dark chocolate budino

200 g (7 oz) dark chocolate pieces***

200 g (7 oz) unsalted butter, cubed

3 x 60 g (2¼ oz) eggs

80 g (2¾ oz) soft brown sugar

1 tablespoon pure maize cornflour (cornstarch)

1 tablespoon unsweetened cocoa powder (I use Dutch cocoa)

additional ingredient

pure icing (confectioners') sugar, to finish

SWEET SECRETS
Bain-marie* — also called a 'water bath'. This is a baking tin in which the pudding moulds are placed and then boiling water is poured into the tin to come halfway up the sides of the moulds.

Dark chocolate pieces*** — I use Nestlé Plaistowe Couverture Deluxe with 63% cocoa pieces

GF vanilla ice cream* and **GF** honeycomb** are available in supermarkets.

place a baking tray lined with freezer wrap in the freezer to chill. This is for the ice-cream balls.

grease 5 x 200 ml (7 fl oz) or 6 x 185 ml (6 fl oz/¾ cup) ramekins or dariole moulds with butter and dust the insides with a combined mixture of 1 tablespoon each unsweetened cocoa powder and pure maize cornflour (cornstarch). Tip moulds upside down and tap over the sink to remove any excess. This helps the pudding to cling to the sides of the moulds and to rise.

preheat oven to 160°C (315°F/Gas 2–3).

place ice cream in a stainless steel bowl and stir in honeycomb to combine. Refreeze. When frozen, scoop balls, place on chilled baking tray and return to the freezer.

place chocolate and butter in a microwave-safe bowl and microwave on medium for 30-second intervals, stirring each time until mixture is smooth and shiny. Cool slightly. Alternatively, place chocolate and butter in a bowl and set over a saucepan of simmering water. Stir until the mixture melts and becomes smooth and shiny.

beat eggs and brown sugar together with an electric mixer in a small bowl until thick and creamy. Add chocolate and butter mixture and beat to combine. Turn mixer down to a low speed.

combine cornflour and cocoa in a small bowl and sift over chocolate mixture. Fold in gently. Fill each mould about three-quarters full. Cover puddings loosely with plastic wrap and refrigerate for about 2 hours (or up to 3 days) before cooking. This helps the puddings to maintain their soft centre during baking.

place puddings in a bain-marie* and bake for about 35 minutes until slightly risen and tops have a crust. The centres should be soft and runny.

serve puddings either in their moulds or turn out onto dessert plates and dust with icing sugar. Serve with cheat's honeycomb ice-cream balls finished with a little reserved crushed honeycomb on top.

fruit with mint & orange marinade

Almost everybody loves fresh fruit salad. It is a refreshing way to finish a meal, especially in the warm summer months. I've added a splash of brandy and the freshness of mint to give this fruit salad a zing. The listed fruit is a guide only. You could use berries only, if you wish.

SERVES 4

250 g (9 oz/1 punnet) strawberries, rinsed, hulled and halved

1 kiwi fruit, peeled and chopped

1 orange or mandarin, peeled, pith removed and segmented

1 sweet red apple, cored and sliced

180 g (6½ oz/1 cup) mixed black and green grapes, cut in half and seeded

1 banana, peeled and sliced

marinade

1 tablespoon brandy or orange-flavoured liqueur, such as Cointreau, Grand Marnier or Triple Sec

1 tablespoon fresh orange juice

1 tablespoon caster (superfine) sugar or runny honey

1 tablespoon baby mint leaves

combine the marinade ingredients in a small bowl and stir well until the sugar has dissolved.

place prepared fruit in a large bowl and pour marinade over. Marinate for about 30 minutes.

serving suggestions

Serve in pretty dessert glasses with **GF** Greek-style yoghurt drizzled with runny honey, whipped cream or **GF** ice cream.

meringues with oranges in star anise syrup

Meringue is such a popular dessert that I just have to include it. The oranges cut the sweetness of the meringue and the boozy star anise syrup gives this dessert quite a kick.

MAKES 6–8

oranges in star anise syrup

4 large oranges, for segments

zest of 2 oranges, finely shredded, and reserved juice

1 large lemon, juice only, strained, you will need a total of 185 ml (6 fl oz/¾ cup) combined orange (from above) and lemon juice

110 g (3¾ oz/½ cup) caster (superfine) sugar

60 ml (2 fl oz/¼ cup) orange-flavoured liqueur, such as Cointreau, Grand Marnier or Triple Sec

1 or 2 star anise

meringues

4 x 60 g (2¼ oz) eggs, whites only, at room temperature

¼ teaspoon cream of tartar

220 g (7¾ oz/1 cup) caster (superfine) sugar

2 teaspoons pure maize cornflour (cornstarch)

1 teaspoon white wine vinegar

additional ingredient

300 ml (10½ fl oz) thickened (whipping) cream, whipped to soft peaks

line a large baking tray with baking paper.

preheat oven to 120°C (235°F/Gas ½).

for the oranges in star anise syrup

place an orange on a chopping board, cut a slice from each end with a small sharp knife. Cut away the peel and the pith working from top to bottom. Segment oranges between the membranes, place in a bowl and set aside. Repeat with remaining 3 oranges.

place the strained orange juice and lemon juice in a small saucepan over medium–high heat. Add orange zest, sugar, liqueur and star anise and boil for 10 minutes to reduce to a syrupy consistency. Set aside to cool.

for the meringues

beat egg whites and cream of tartar with an electric mixer until soft peaks form. Add 75 g (2¾ oz/⅓ cup) sugar and beat for 3 minutes. Add remaining sugar, 1 tablespoon at a time, beating well after each addition until sugar has dissolved and meringue is thick and glossy. Sift cornflour over meringue and add vinegar, folding in gently.

heap 6–8 large dollops of meringue, using two large spoons, onto the baking tray and draw meringue up into peaks. Alternatively use a piping (icing) bag to pipe the meringues. Bake for 1 hour or until dry to the touch. Turn oven off, leaving the meringues in the oven with the door shut for 1 hour as this will help prevent surface cracking.

serve meringues with dollops of whipped cream and orange segments with star anise syrup.

SWEET SECRETS

Rub a little meringue between your thumb and finger. If the texture is grainy, continue beating until the sugar dissolves. You can substitute tangelos for oranges.

To vary the meringue, add citrus zest to the mixture.

If you freeze egg whites, you will require 115 g (4 oz) for the recipe above. Defrost egg whites and use at room temperature.

parisian macarons

When I need a reminder of my trips to Paris I whip up a batch of these fabulous almond macarons. Once you've made parisian macarons you will not only want to eat them often, you will possibly make Paris your next holiday destination.

MAKES 48
(24 PAIRED MACARONS)

ganache

125 g (4½ oz) **GF** dark chocolate pieces*

80 ml (2½ fl oz/⅓ cup) thickened (whipping) cream

chocolate macarons

185 g (6½ oz/1½ cups) pure icing (confectioners') sugar

2½ tablespoons unsweetened cocoa powder (I use Dutch cocoa)

125 g (4½ oz/1¼ cups) ground almonds

3 x 60 g (2¼ oz) eggs, whites only, at room temperature

pinch of salt

2 tablespoons caster (superfine) sugar

SWEET SECRETS

GF dark chocolate pieces*—I use Nestlé Plaistowe Couverture Deluxe with 63% cocoa pieces. It is available in supermarkets.

Macarons may be frozen filled or unfilled, and stored in an airtight container. I'm usually impatient and eat them straight from the freezer!

line two baking trays with double layers of baking paper.

preheat oven to 130°C (250°F/Gas 1).

for the ganache

place chocolate and cream in a microwave-safe bowl and microwave on medium for 30-second intervals, stirring each time until mixture is smooth and shiny. Set aside to cool. Alternatively, place chocolate and cream in a bowl and set over a saucepan of simmering water. Stir until the mixture melts and becomes smooth and shiny.

for the chocolate macarons

sift icing sugar and cocoa together then stir in ground almonds to combine. Set aside.

whisk egg whites and salt with an electric mixer until soft peaks form. Add sugar gradually and beat well. Rub a little meringue between thumb and finger. If the texture is grainy, continue beating until sugar has dissolved. Fold combined icing sugar mixture gradually into egg mixture, using the lowest setting on the mixer. It does not matter that the mixture loses volume.

spoon about half of the mixture into a piping (icing) bag fitted with a 1.5 cm (⅝ inch) nozzle. To support the piping bag, rest it in a jug while filling. Twist or fold the top of the bag down. Pipe 3 cm (1¼ inch) rounds onto the prepared baking trays, holding the piping bag about 1 cm (½ inch) above the baking paper and gently squeezing bag from the top. Lift the piping bag up and away from the macaron. Refill piping bag with remaining mixture and repeat.

hold trays one at a time 30 cm (12 inches) above your work surface and drop them down with a bang. This is to spread the macarons a little. Set aside at room temperature for at least 15 minutes. Bake one tray at a time for about 20 minutes until top is lightly crisp and the centre soft. Cool macarons on trays, they will firm a little more as they cool.

pair similar-sized macarons before sandwiching together with ganache. Using a butter knife, spread a small amount of ganache on the flat side of a macaron and place its pair on top.

potted cream with caramel

These little pots are so scrumptious you will not believe just how easy they are to prepare. They are ready in a flash and sit patiently in the refrigerator until you are ready to serve. The brown sugar creates caramel syrup in the base and on top of the potted cream. Yum!

SERVES 6

75 g (2¾ oz) soft brown sugar

250 ml (9 fl oz/1 cup) thickened (whipping) cream

750 g (1 lb 10 oz/3 cups) **GF** Greek-style yoghurt

vanilla bean paste or natural vanilla extract, to taste

sprinkle 1 teaspoon of brown sugar in the base of 6 x 200 ml (7 fl oz) dessert glasses or ramekins.

whisk cream lightly until soft peaks form using an electric mixer or balloon whisk. Fold in yoghurt and vanilla. Spoon mixture into glasses or ramekins and sprinkle tops with remaining brown sugar. Cover with plastic wrap and refrigerate. The yoghurt and cream mixture will thicken and the sugar will become syrupy.

serving suggestions
Prepare or buy a delicate biscuit to serve with the potted cream. Alternatively, serve with strawberries, poached apples, apricots or pears.

SWEET SECRETS
This dessert can be prepared up to 4 hours in advance.

Vary the recipe by adding diced banana to the mixture. If you add bananas, you will make 1 or 2 extra desserts depending on how much banana you add.

shortbread sweethearts

Shortbread is generally a Christmas biscuit (cookie) but why wait until the festive season to enjoy this melt-in-the-mouth treat?

MAKES APPROXIMATELY 36

125 g (4½ oz) unsalted butter, softened

60 g (2¼ oz/½ cup) pure icing (confectioners') sugar

vanilla bean paste or natural vanilla extract, to taste

70 g (2½ oz) pure maize cornflour (cornstarch)

90 g (3¼ oz/½ cup) white rice flour

60 g (2¼ oz/½ cup) tapioca flour

caster (superfine) sugar, for sprinkling (optional)

pure icing (confectioners') sugar, for dusting

line two baking trays with baking paper.

preheat oven to 170°C (325°F/Gas 3).

cream butter in a food processor. Add the icing sugar and vanilla and whizz to blend well.

sift flours together and add to processor. Whizz briefly, then pulse (turn off and on action) until the dough begins to come together.

turn dough onto a sheet of baking paper and bring together with your hands. Flatten slightly. Cover with a second sheet of baking paper and use a rolling pin to roll the dough out to approximately 5 mm (¼ inch) thickness. Place on a tray and refrigerate for 30 minutes to firm before cutting.

cut out shortbreads with heart-shaped pastry cutters (or other shape of your choice). Place shortbreads on prepared trays leaving some space between the biscuits as they will spread a little. Sprinkle with caster sugar, if desired.

bake one tray at a time for about 8 minutes or until shortbreads are lightly coloured. Transfer to a wire rack to cool. Store in an airtight container.

serve dusted with icing sugar.

SWEET SECRETS
Shortbread will keep in an airtight container for about 1 week.

To vary the recipe, add spice, citrus zest, instant coffee granules, finely chopped nuts or chocolate chips to the dough.

Drizzle shortbread with melted chocolate for an extra special treat.

st clement's jelly

'"Oranges and lemons" say the bells of St Clement's' ... As a child I recall my mother making jelly, usually the commercial kind, for our birthday parties. The jelly was set in orange halves. My recipe is refreshing and has a lot less sugar than commercial jelly. Even adults will enjoy it, particularly with a dash of liqueur added!

MAKES APPROXIMATELY
700 ML (24 FL OZ)

60 ml (2 fl oz/¼ cup) warm water

1 tablespoon powdered gelatine

100 ml (3½ fl oz) boiling water

115 g (4 oz/½ cup) sugar (use less if oranges are very sweet)

4–6 oranges to make 400 ml (14 fl oz) orange juice, strained (remove pulp from orange half-shells and reserve for setting and serving, if desired)

place warm water in a small microwave-safe bowl and sprinkle gelatine over the top. Allow gelatine to soften for 1 minute before placing in microwave. Heat on medium for 40 seconds, stir well and then microwave for another 15 seconds or until gelatine has dissolved. Stir well. Alternatively follow instructions on the packet to dissolve gelatine.

place boiling water and sugar in a saucepan over medium heat and stir until sugar has dissolved. Alternatively, you can also place the boiling water and sugar in a microwave-safe bowl and heat on high for 1–2 minutes until sugar has dissolved.

add dissolved gelatine and orange juice to the sugar syrup and stir well. Pour into jelly moulds, set in a bowl or in orange shells-halves. Place orange shells to rest in the holes of a muffin tray, as this will hold them steady. Place jelly in refrigerator to set.

SWEET SECRETS
To vary the recipe, substitute lemon juice for the orange juice and adjust sugar to taste. Prepare jelly recipe as above.

For an adult-only jelly, reduce the amount of boiling water by 1 tablespoon and add 1 tablespoon of orange-flavoured liqueur (such as Cointreau, Grand Marnier or Triple Sec). Serve with **oranges in star anise syrup** (page 178) or **fruit with mint & orange marinade** (page 176).

summer berry puddings

I like to make individual summer berry puddings as they look quite special when plated.

MAKES 6

18 slices **GF** firm plain bread (I use Country Life Bakery gluten-free bread)

400 g (14 oz) strawberries, rinsed, hulled and cut into quarters

400 g (14 oz) fresh or frozen raspberries

400 g (14 oz) fresh or frozen blueberries

125 g (4½ oz/1 cup) pure icing (confectioners') sugar

185 ml (6 fl oz/¾ cup) boiling water

185 ml (6 fl oz/¾ cup) orange-flavoured liqueur, such as Cointreau, Grand Marnier or Triple Sec

3 teaspoons lemon juice

3 teaspoons arrowroot

SWEET SECRETS

If you are short of berry syrup, heat a few more raspberries in sugar and water to produce extra. Strain the berries before using the syrup.

After cutting the **GF** bread into shapes for the puddings, process any offcuts to make breadcrumbs. Freeze **GF** breadcrumbs to use in other recipes.

line six 200 ml (7 fl oz) pudding moulds with freezer or plastic wrap, leaving plenty overhanging the rims.

cut three slices of bread for the base into rounds using a 5.5 cm (2¼ inch) diameter cutter. Cut each round in half horizontally so that you now have six rounds. Set aside.

cut three slices of bread for the tops of the pudding into rounds using a 6.5 cm (2¾ inch) diameter cutter. Cut each round in half horizontally so that you now have six rounds. Set aside.

cut the remaining 12 slices of bread into squares using a square 6 cm x 6 cm (2½ x 2½ inch) cutter. Cut each square in half horizontally so that you now have 24 squares of bread. Set aside.

combine berries, icing sugar, boiling water and liqueur in a saucepan. Marinate the berries for 30 minutes. Place pan over low heat and simmer for 2 minutes. Add lemon juice. Strain berries and reserve berries and syrup.

dip a round of bread for the base in the syrup and place in each pudding mould. Dip one square of bread at a time in the syrup and line the inside of each mould with four slightly overlapping squares of bread. Fill moulds with reserved berries.

strain remaining syrup into a small saucepan and heat gently. Make a paste with arrowroot and 2 tablespoons cool water and stir into syrup. It will thicken slightly. Pour thickened syrup over berries, filling to the top of the moulds.

place a round of bread on top of each pudding. Spoon remaining syrup over lid. Fold over-hanging freezer or plastic wrap over the puddings to fully enclose.

place puddings on a tray to catch any drips of juice, then place a flat heavy dish on top to press down the puddings. Refrigerate overnight.

unfold freezer or plastic wrap. Turn pudding upside down on a dessert plate. Remove freezer or plastic wrap. Serve with fresh berries or **berry sauce** (page 194).

upside-down pear or apple cake

Serve this cake for dessert or prepare **afternoon teacake**. See sweet secrets below.

MAKES 8–10 GENEROUS PIECES

caramelised pears or apples

60 g (2¼ oz) unsalted butter

60 g (2¼ oz) caster (superine) sugar

800 g (1 lb 12 oz) beurre bosc pears or granny smith apples, peeled, cored and quartered or sliced

1 tablespoon brandy (optional)

cake

40 g (1½ oz/⅓ cup) tapioca flour

115 g (4 oz/⅔ cup) white rice flour

40 g (1½ oz/¼ cup) buckwheat flour

40 g (1½ oz/⅓ cup) pure maize cornflour (cornstarch)

1 teaspoon ground cinnamon

1 teaspoon **GF** baking powder

¼ teaspoon bicarbonate of soda (baking soda)

100 g (3½ oz/1 cup) ground almonds

125 g (4½ oz) unsalted butter, softened

145 g (5¼ oz/⅔ cup) caster (superfine) sugar

½ teaspoon natural vanilla extract

zest of 1 lemon, finely grated and reserving 1 tablespoon juice or brandy

3 x 60 g (2¼ oz) eggs

125 g (4½ oz/½ cup) **GF** Greek-style yoghurt

line the base and side of a 24 cm (9½ inch) round cake tin with baking paper.

preheat oven to 180°C (350°F/Gas 4).

melt butter and sugar in a heavy-based frying pan over medium–high heat. Add pears or apples and cook for 15 minutes or until they have caramelised, then add brandy and cook briefly. Spread caramelised pears or apples over the base of the cake tin.

sift flours, cinnamon, baking powder and bicarbonate of soda together and stir in the ground almonds.

beat butter, sugar, vanilla and lemon zest in a small bowl with an electric mixer until creamy. Add eggs one at a time beating well after each addition.

fold in half the sifted ingredients then stir in yoghurt and lemon juice. Fold in remaining sifted ingredients and gently combine.

spoon cake batter on top of pears or apples and smooth the top.

bake for 40–45 minutes or until done when tested with a skewer which should come out clean. Stand in pan for 10 minutes, then invert cake onto a serving plate.

serving suggestions

Serve with **caramel sauce** (page 194) (optional), mascarpone cheese or sweetened whipped cream.

SWEET SECRETS

This cake may be made in advance and reheated in the microwave.

To make **afternoon teacake** omit caramelised fruit and bake cake mixture as above. When cake is cooked, brush top of cake with 1 tablespoon melted butter and sprinkle with a combined mixture of 2 teaspoons caster (superfine) sugar and ½ teaspoon ground cinnamon.

SAUCES AND BASICS

sauces

These sweet sauces can make a gluten-free cake, crepes or ice cream into a special treat.
They appeared in my first cookbook *Sharing Sweet Secrets: Gluten & Wheat free*.

berry sauce

MAKES 250 ML (9 FL OZ/1 CUP)

350 g (12 oz/2⅓ cups) strawberries, rinsed and hulled,
or fresh or frozen raspberries, thawed

30 g (1 oz/¼ cup) pure icing (confectioners') sugar

2 teaspoons strained lemon juice

place ingredients in a food processor and blend thoroughly
until smooth.

press purée through a sieve to remove the berry seeds.
Discard seeds. Thin the sauce with a little water if necessary.
Store in the refrigerator for up to 2 days.

caramel sauce

MAKES 250 ML (9 FL OZ/1 CUP)

50 g (1¾ oz) unsalted butter, cubed

125 ml (4 fl oz/½ cup) thickened (whipping) cream

95 g (3¼ oz/½ cup) lightly packed soft brown sugar

place ingredients in a microwave-safe bowl and microwave
on medium for 90 seconds. Alternatively place ingredients
in a small saucepan over low–medium heat. Stir until the
mixture melts.

blend with a hand-held blender or whisk until smooth.
Store in the refrigerator for up to 1 week.

chocolate glaze

Use this glaze to top small cakes or choux pastries.

MAKES 125 ML (4 FL OZ/½ CUP)

40 g (1½ oz) unsalted butter, cubed
80 g (2¾ oz) dark chocolate pieces*

combine ingredients in a small microwave-safe bowl and microwave on medium for 30-second intervals stirring each time until chocolate is melted. Alternatively place chocolate and butter in a bowl and set over a saucepan of simmering water. Stir until the mixture melts and becomes smooth and shiny. Store in the refrigerator for up to 1 week.

SWEET SECRET
GF dark chocolate pieces* I use Nestlé Plaistowe Couverture Deluxe with 63% cocoa pieces, it is available in supermarkets.

passionfruit sauce

Serve this sauce over meringues and cream, in trifles or with panna cotta.

MAKES 125 ML (4 FL OZ/½ CUP)

3 large passionfruit, cut in half and pulp removed and reserved
60 ml (2 fl oz/¼ cup) orange juice, strained
2 tablespoons caster (superfine) sugar
1 teaspoon arrowroot mixed with 2 teaspoons water

simmer pulp, orange juice and sugar in a small saucepan over low–medium heat until the sugar is just dissolved. Strain mixture over a bowl. Discard approximately half the seeds. Return juice and remaining seeds to saucepan.

whisk in the arrowroot paste and warm gently, continuing to whisk until sauce thickens slightly. Store in the refrigerator for up to 1 week.

chicken stock

Homemade stock is far superior in flavour and health benefits to any commercial product. It is cheap and easy to make too. You can prepare this stock one of two ways, depending on whether you want a pale coloured or a light brown chicken stock.

MAKES APPROXIMATELY 3 LITRES
(105 FL OZ/12 CUPS)

2 chicken carcasses or 1 kg (2 lb 4 oz) chicken necks

1 large white onion, skin on and chopped

2 carrots, unpeeled and chopped

2 celery stalks, chopped

1 garlic clove, sliced

10 black peppercorns

2 bay leaves

1 handful herbs, a mix of parsley, thyme, oregano and rosemary

place all ingredients in a stockpot. Cover with cold water and bring to the boil over high heat. Immediately reduce heat to low and simmer, uncovered, for 2 hours. Skim and discard any froth that rises to the surface.

cool stock quickly see **cook's tips — cooling** (page 211). Remove bones and solids with tongs before straining stock through a fine sieve into a large bowl. Discard bones and solids. Refrigerate stock when cool. Fat will solidify on the surface. Remove fat and discard.

reduce chicken stock by bringing to the boil again over high heat. Partially cover and boil rapidly. Reduce stock by half or more to concentrate the flavour.

SAVOURY SECRETS

Chicken stock can be used in sauces, soups, casseroles, risotto and pilaff.

Freeze stock in containers or zip-lock bags.

To make **light brown chicken stock** place chicken carcasses or necks, 1 brown onion, skin on and chopped, 2 carrots and 2 tomatoes in a roasting tin and drizzle with oil. Bake for about 45 minutes at 180°C (350°F/Gas 4) until chicken bones brown and vegetables caramelise. Transfer to a large stockpot. Pour about 250 ml (17 fl oz/1 cup) water into the roasting tin and stir to scrape up any brown residue from the base.
Add this liquid to the stockpot along with celery, garlic, peppercorns, bay leaves and herbs (as per main recipe). Cover with cold water and follow instructions above.

beef stock

Stock adds flavour and richness to sauces, soups and casseroles. I like to use some of this stock to make **demi-glaze** (page 198). You can use one large stockpot or two medium-sized stockpots. I find it easier to lift and handle two pots.

MAKES ABOUT 5 LITRES
(175 FL OZ/20 CUPS) STOCK OR 2 LITRES
(70 FL OZ/8 CUPS) REDUCED STOCK

3–4 kg (6 lb 12 oz–9 lb) beef bones

60 ml (2 fl oz/¼ cup) vegetable oil

2 brown onions, skin on and chopped

2 carrots, unpeeled and chopped

2 celery stalks, chopped

2 garlic cloves, chopped

250 g (9 oz) gravy beef (or other stewing steak)

150 g (5½ oz) **GF** bacon (optional)

4 tablespoons **GF** tomato paste (concentrated purée)

3–4 bay leaves

10 black peppercorns

1 very large handful herbs, such as parsley, sage, rosemary, thyme and oregano, tied in a bundle with cooking twine

SAVOURY SECRETS

Freeze stock in containers or zip-lock bags.

For a more intense flavour, add some mushrooms to the stockpot when sautéing the vegetables.

Prepare stocks and demi-glazes the day before your garbage is collected so bones are not sitting around in the garbage bin for days. Or freeze bones and place in garbage just before it is taken away.

preheat oven to 200°C (400°F/Gas 6).

place beef bones in a single layer in one or two roasting tins. Bake for 20 minutes. Turn beef bones and bake for a further 20 minutes or until bones are very brown but not burnt. Pour off rendered fat and discard.

heat oil in a stockpot, add onion, carrot and celery and cook over medium heat for about 8 minutes stirring often until well caramelised but not too brown. Add garlic and cook briefly. Remove vegetables to a bowl and set aside. Add gravy beef and bacon to pot and brown well. Add 500 ml (17 fl oz/2 cups) water to the pot and bring to the boil. Stir and scrape up any brown residue from the base of the pot. (If using two pots divide the mixture at this point.) Add beef bones, vegetables, tomato paste, bay leaves, peppercorns and herbs to pot/s.

pour 250 ml (9 fl oz/1 cup) water into the roasting tin/s in which the bones were browned, place over medium–high heat and bring to the boil. Stir and scrape up any brown residue from the base and pour into pot/s. Fill pot/s with cold water and bring to the boil. Reduce heat to low and gently simmer, partially cover and cook for a minimum of 5 hours. Skim and discard any froth that rises to the surface. This will give you a clear stock.

cool stock quickly see **cook's tips — cooling** (page 211). Remove bones with tongs before straining stock through a fine sieve into a large bowl. Discard bones and solids. Refrigerate stock when cool. Fat will solidify on the surface. Remove fat and discard.

reduce stock by bringing to the boil again over high heat. Partially cover and boil rapidly. Reduce stock by half or more to concentrate the flavour. This will take approximately 45 minutes. Cool stock.

stock can be frozen in portions at this point or reduced down further to make a deliciously rich **demi-glaze** (page 198).

demi-glaze

This is a superb sauce to serve with beef or lamb. It elevates a simple steak or rack of lamb to a special meal.

MAKES APPROXIMATELY 20 X 1 TABLE-
SPOON (20 ML) SINGLE SERVES

2 litres (8 cups) reduced **beef stock** (page 197)

500 ml (17 fl oz/2 cups) good-quality red wine

125 ml (4 fl oz/½ cup) port

place beef stock into a large saucepan or small stockpot over high heat and bring to the boil.

add red wine and port and boil rapidly. Skim and discard any froth that rises to the surface. Reduce liquid to 500 ml (17 fl oz/2 cups) demi-glaze.

cool and refrigerate or freeze.

SAVOURY SECRETS
You can make a paste with arrowroot and cool water and add it to the demi-glaze to thicken slightly.

Freeze demi-glaze in ice-cube trays. Transfer frozen cubes to zip-lock bags.

caramelised shallot sauce

French shallots are small brown onions and are also known as eschalots. They have a delicate flavour and aroma. Larger French shallots are known as pickling onions.

SERVES 2

300 g (10½ oz) French shallots (eschalots)

15 g (½ oz) unsalted butter

1 garlic clove, crushed

2 tablespoons raspberry vinegar

1 tablespoon balsamic vinegar

185 ml (6 fl oz/¾ cup) **GF** chicken or **GF** beef stock

2 teaspoons soft brown sugar

1 teaspoon redcurrant jelly

1 bay leaf

½ teaspoon mixed dried herbs

cover shallots with boiling water and leave for 5 minutes. Drain, then peel once cooled slightly and cut any large shallots in half.

melt butter in a small frying pan over medium heat, add shallots and cook until lightly browned. Add garlic and cook briefly then add remaining ingredients. Season with freshly ground black pepper and bring to the boil. Reduce heat to low and simmer to reduce liquid to a syrupy consistency. This will take about 20 minutes. The shallots should be meltingly soft and caramelised.

serving suggestion
Serve with pan-fried or barbecued steaks, lamb or hamburgers.

easy tomato sauce

The quality of tinned tomatoes varies considerably. I use tinned Italian roma (plum) tomatoes.

MAKES APPROXIMATELY
500 ML (17 FL OZ/2 CUPS)

3 teaspoons olive oil

1 small onion, finely diced

1 garlic clove, crushed

2 bay leaves

400 g (14 oz) tin chopped tomatoes

2 teaspoons **GF** tomato paste
(concentrated purée)

1 teaspoon sugar

1 teaspoon balsamic vinegar

heat a frying pan over medium heat. Add olive oil and sauté the onion for about 4 minutes or until softened. Add garlic and cook briefly.

add bay leaves, tomato, 250 ml (9 fl oz/1 cup) water*, tomato paste, sugar and vinegar. Season with salt and freshly ground black pepper and bring to the boil. Reduce heat to a rapid simmer and cook sauce for about 25 minutes, stirring occasionally until it thickens.

SAVOURY SECRETS

Rinse tomato tin with the water*.

Simply by adding a few ingredients to this sauce you can have a meal ready very quickly. Here are a few suggestions: herbs, anchovies, capers, mozzarella, **GF** chorizo sausage, chicken, seafood and **GF** meatballs. You can also cook stuffed vegetables such as eggplant (aubergines), capsicum (peppers) and zucchini (courgettes) in the sauce. It is also great served with **GF** pasta, polenta and **GF** crepes.

To make **tomato mascarpone & basil dip** prepare **easy tomato sauce,** omitting water from the method. Cook sauce for 10 minutes, add 2 or 3 tablespoons mascarpone cheese and a generous amount of fresh basil or any other herb you have to hand. Transfer to a food processor and whizz briefly so that the dip retains its chunky texture. Serve warm or cold.

Freeze the sauce in portions.

whole-egg mayonnaise

Mayonnaise is very simple to make especially with a food processor. I must admit that I have on occasions resorted to my **cheat's lime mayonnaise** (see savoury secrets below).

MAKES ABOUT 250 G
(9 OZ/1 CUP)

1 x 60 g (2¼ oz) egg, at room temperature

100 ml (3½ fl oz) light olive oil

80 ml (2½ fl oz/⅓ cup) grape seed oil or vegetable oil

1 garlic clove, crushed

1 teaspoon **GF** dijon mustard

2 teaspoons lemon juice

1 teaspoon white wine vinegar

break egg into a food processor and add 1 tablespoon olive oil. Whizz to blend.

place remaining olive oil and grape seed oil in a jug. With processor motor running, drip about a quarter of the combined oil through the feed tube. The mayonnaise will begin to thicken. Now gradually pour the remaining oil through the feed tube in a steady stream. Add a little more oil for a thicker mayonnaise.

add garlic, mustard, lemon juice and vinegar. Season with salt and freshly ground black pepper and whizz well to combine.

SAVOURY SECRETS

Whole-egg mayonnaise will keep for 1 week in the refrigerator in an airtight container.

To thin the mayonnaise, add a little hot water, vinaigrette or **GF** chicken stock.

Add puréed **roasted red capsicums** (page 164) to mayonnaise to serve with prawns (shrimp) or crayfish.

Add a teaspoon of harissa paste to mayonnaise to serve with **GF** hamburgers.

To make **cheat's lime mayonnaise** purchase **GF** whole-egg mayonnaise, add crushed garlic, **GF** dijon mustard and zest and juice of 1 lime. Whisk to blend.

To make **quick dressing for potato salad** combine equal quantities of **GF** mayonnaise and **GF** Greek-style yoghurt or sour cream, add chopped spring onions (scallions), capers and the finely grated zest and juice of 1 lemon.

To make **quick tartare sauce** add 3 tablespoons each chopped capers, gherkins (pickles) and parsley plus 1 finely chopped spring onion (scallion) to 250 g (9 oz/1 cup) **GF** whole-egg mayonnaise. Stir to blend.

preserved lemons

If you have a lemon tree it is really worth preserving the fruit in salt. It is quick and easy to do. Preserved lemons enhance so many dishes, from salads and vegetables, fish and chicken to slow-cooked meaty casseroles. If you are purchasing lemons, try to buy unsprayed, unwaxed organic lemons.

MAKES 6 X 300 ML
(10½ FL OZ)

350 g (12 oz) coarse cooking salt

150 g (5½ oz) rock salt (sea salt crystals)

10 –12 lemons rinsed and cut into quarters

6 bay leaves

5 lemons, extra, to yield 250 ml
(9 fl oz/1 cup) juice

combine coarse cooking salt and rock salt in a large stainless steel, glass or plastic bowl.

place 1 tablespoon of combined salt into each of 6 x 300 ml (10½ fl oz) sterilised jars with lids.

add lemon wedges to the bowl of salt and coat well.

pack salt-crusted lemon wedges into jars, peel-side facing out and insert a bay leaf into each jar. Press down hard on the wedges to release some of the juice. Spoon all of the remaining salt between the jars.

pour in lemon juice to cover. Using a clean cloth dipped in boiling water wipe around the neck of the jars to remove any salt. Screw jar lid in place.

leave lemons to mature for at least 1 month but preferably 6 weeks before using. Store preserved lemons in a cool place (not in the refrigerator), to mature. Once a jar of preserved lemons is opened, store in the refrigerator.

SAVOURY SECRETS

To sterilise jars and lids* place on the hot rinse cycle in the dishwasher.

Shake and invert jars several times during the first week of maturation.

Occasionally a white mould may develop on a piece of lemon that has not been covered with lemon juice. This mould is harmless. Discard mould and continue to use lemons.

Preserved lemons last for more than a year.

To use preserved lemons, discard pulp, rinse the rind and chop or slice according to recipe.

Generally there is no need to add salt to a recipe if using preserved lemons.

To make **preserved lemon butter** mash 1 tablespoon of rinsed preserved lemon rind with 50 g (1¾ oz) unsalted butter and serve with fish or grilled chicken.

cheesy soft polenta

Polenta can have a soft consistency as in this recipe or can be left to firm and then grilled or finished in the oven as in **polenta pizza bites** (page 24).

SERVES 4–6

90 g (3¼ oz) coarse polenta

90 g (3¼ oz) fine (one-minute) polenta

500 ml (17 fl oz/2 cups) milk

500 ml (17 fl oz/2 cups) **GF** chicken or **GF** vegetable stock

55 g (2 oz) grated parmesan cheese

100 g (3½ oz) Fontina cheese, thinly sliced

combine coarse and fine polenta and set aside.

place milk and stock in a large saucepan over high heat and bring to the boil.

pour combined polenta into the liquid in a thin, steady stream. Reduce heat to low–medium and stir continuously with a wooden spoon for 3 minutes.

add cheeses and stir well until they melt into the polenta.

serve polenta as you would mashed potato.

serving suggestion
Serve with **orange marmalade duck ragout** (page 90). Alternatively, you can serve as a starter with **roasted red capsicum** (page 164), grilled prosciutto or pancetta and toasted pine nuts. Weave prosciutto onto metal skewers before grilling to achieve a crinkled effect. Be careful not to burn your fingers when removing prosciutto from hot skewers.

SAVOURY SECRET
To vary the recipe, add chopped herbs.

quinoa

Quinoa, pronounced 'keenwa', is a superfood with more protein than any other grain. It has a delicious nutty flavour and can be served simply with a squeeze of lemon or jazzed up with other ingredients. Serve quinoa as you would rice.

SERVES 4

200g (7oz/1 cup) quinoa, rinsed

cook quinoa by absorption method according to directions on the packet. Substitute **GF** chicken stock for water.

SAVOURY SECRETS

Add lemon zest or chopped preserved lemon rin, coriander (cilantro) leaves or parsley and finely chopped or sliced spring onions (scallions). Pine nuts or almonds add texture too.

You can purchase natural, red and black quinoa from supermarkets or health food stores.

You can cook quinoa in advance. It reheats well in the microwave.

To make **quinoa with chickpeas** add drained and rinsed tinned chickpeas to cooked quinoa. Heat through and serve with Moroccan-style recipes.

To make **quinoa tabouleh** combine 2 cups cooked quinoa, 1 cup each diced tomato and cucumber, 4 chopped spring onions (scallions) and 1 cup combined chopped parsley and mint in a large bowl. Season with salt and freshly ground black pepper. For the dressing, whisk 1 crushed garlic clove, 2 tablespoons lemon juice and 2 tablespoons olive oil together in a small bowl. Mix dressing lightly through the tabouleh.

saffron pilaff with vermicelli

The combination of rice with vermicelli gives a very nice texture to pilaff. You can serve it with fish, seafood, chicken, duck or lamb. I particularly like it served with lamb that has been rubbed with a blend of Moroccan spices then pan-fried or barbecued.

SERVES 4

55 g (2 oz) dried rice vermicelli

750 ml (26 fl oz/3 cups) boiling water

400 ml (14 fl oz) **GF** chicken stock

generous pinch of saffron threads

1 tablespoon olive oil

10 g (¼ oz) unsalted butter

4 spring onions (scallions) or 1 leek, white part only, trimmed, rinsed well and thinly sliced

1 garlic clove, crushed

200 g (7 oz/1 cup) basmati rice, rinsed well

125 ml (4 fl oz/½ cup) dry white wine

2 makrut (kaffir lime) leaves

place vermicelli in a bowl and cover with boiling water. Leave to soften for 10 minutes while you cook the pilaff. Stir vermicelli occasionally with a fork to separate noodles.

heat stock and saffron in a saucepan over medium heat until simmering.

heat oil and butter in a large heavy-based saucepan (with a tight-fitting lid) over medium heat. Add spring onion and garlic and sauté until softened. Add rice and stir for 1 minute then add wine. Allow wine to boil and cook until it has almost evaporated. Add hot stock, lime leaves and season with salt. Reduce heat to very low and cook covered for 14 minutes or until rice is cooked. No peeking until the end of cooking time!

drain vermicelli well and cut through noodles several times with a knife or kitchen scissors. Add to pilaff, stir through and cover with the lid. Turn heat off and leave for 10 minutes before serving.

SAVOURY SECRETS
Prepare pilaff in advance and reheat in a microwave.

If you use a **GF** stock cube you may not need to add salt to the pilaff.

You can omit the vermicelli from the pilaff altogether.

To vary the pilaff, add coriander (cilantro) leaves, raisins or sliced dried apricots, and toasted almonds or pine nuts after the pilaff is cooked.

fail-proof choux pastry

People seem to squirm when it comes to making pastry, especially choux pastry. It really is so easy and versatile too. What could be more delicious than a delicate éclair or profiterole filled with custard and berries? This choux is suitable for sweet and savoury fillings.

MAKES APPROXIMATELY 24 X 5 CM
(2 INCH) MINI ÉCLAIRS

35 g (1¼ oz/¼ cup) **GF** plain (all-purpose) flour*

45 g (1¾ oz/¼ cup) white rice flour

55 g (2 oz) unsalted butter, cut into small cubes

2 x 60 g (2¼ oz) eggs

1 egg yolk, extra

fit a piping (icing) bag with a 1.5 cm (⅝ inch) nozzle to pipe eclairs or use two spoons to make puffs.

line two baking trays with baking paper.

preheat oven to 200°C (400°F/Gas 6).

sift flours together, then sift again.

place 125 ml (4 fl oz/½ cup) water and the butter in a small saucepan and boil over high heat until butter melts. Add flour all at once and stir quickly with a wooden spoon to incorporate. Remove from heat and beat vigorously until smooth. It will look gluey. Return saucepan to a very low heat for a few seconds and continue to beat until the paste comes away from the side of the saucepan.

transfer choux batter to a food processor and whizz for 10 seconds. Add eggs one at a time, processing well after each addition. Process choux until it becomes smooth and shiny.

pipe éclairs or spoon walnut-sized portions onto baking trays.

whisk extra egg yolk with 1 tablespoon water in a small bowl using a fork. Glaze tops of choux with a pastry brush.

bake for 20–25 minutes until puffed, crisp and golden brown. Place on a wire rack to cool.

SAVOURY SECRETS
GF plain flour* I use either F.G. Roberts gluten-free plain flour or Orgran gluten-free all-purpose plain flour. Both flours are available in some supermarkets and health food stores.

Mini éclairs are suitable to use for party food nibbles especially **éclairs with smoked salmon & horseradish cream** (page 20).

Prepare fail-proof choux pastry to make **chorizo parsley puffs** (page 16).

herbed crepes

Crepes are so versatile. They can be eaten as a starter, main course or dessert (omit herbs for sweet crepes of course!). Try my **herbed crepes with spinach & ricotta** (page 116) or **crepe lasagne** (page 104).

MAKES 8

150 g (5½ oz/1 cup) **GF** plain flour*

2 x 60 g (2¼ oz) eggs

310 ml (10¾ fl oz/1¼ cups) milk plus a little more to thin batter, if necessary

20 g (¾ oz) unsalted butter, melted

1 tablespoon chopped flat-leaf (Italian) parsley

unsalted butter, for frying

place flour, eggs, milk and melted butter in a food processor and whizz to blend until smooth. Add parsley and whizz briefly.

heat a 24 cm (9½ inch) non-stick crepe pan over medium–high heat and grease lightly with a little of the additional butter. Pour 60 ml (2 fl oz/¼ cup) batter into the pan. Tilt and swirl pan to distribute batter evenly over the base.

cook until top of crepe sets and edges begin to turn golden brown. Turn crepe and cook the other side for 30 seconds. Slide crepe from pan onto a wire rack or plate.

add a little more butter to the pan. Whisk batter between making each crepe. Continue to cook crepes until all of the batter is used.

SAVOURY SECRETS

GF plain flour* I use either F.G. Roberts gluten-free plain flour or Orgran gluten-free all-purpose flour. Both flours are available in some supermarkets and health food stores.

Crepes may be made by using a whisk, food processor or electric mixer.

Crepes may be prepared in advance. They can be layered with freezer wrap and enclosed in foil or zip-lock bags. Before using crepes, allow them to defrost then microwave each crepe for 10 seconds on high heat to make them more pliable.

COOK'S TIPS

bay leaves

These leaves, whether dried or fresh, are used in many recipes. Plant a bay tree (*Laurus nobilis*) in a pot so that you have a constant supply of these aromatic evergreen leaves. They are used to flavour stock, soups and casseroles and of course are essential in a bouquet garni. To release more flavour from fresh bay leaves, make a tear in the leaves before adding to a dish.

beef, lamb & pork

Marinate meat before freezing. Defrost in the refrigerator when required.

bread

Freeze a loaf of **GF** bread in portions. Wrap two slices of bread (per portion) in plastic wrap. You can then take the required number of slices from the freezer without having to take the whole loaf out each time.

Save crusts from **GF** bread and when you have about half a dozen, process them in a food processor and store crumbs in a zip-lock bag in the freezer. Alternatively process a whole or half-loaf of day-old bread into crumbs and freeze.

Use **GF** breadcrumbs for crumbles, crusts, stuffing for fish, pork or chicken balls, coating fish or chicken breasts. There are many desserts in which they are used too. Any recipe that calls for 'normal wheaten' breadcrumbs can be made with **GF** breadcrumbs.

Make **GF** breadcrumb stuffing for your Christmas turkey up to a month in advance. Freeze the stuffing so that all you have to do is defrost it in the refrigerator the day before it is required. See **craisin & pistachio stuffing** (page 96).

If you are crumbing fish or chicken, prepare extra and freeze flat. Wrap well in plastic wrap and seal in containers or zip-lock bags. You can prepare cubed or strips of fish and chicken for finger food this way too.

butter

Cut butter into cubes to have ready for pan-frying. Store cubes in a zip-lock bag.

Prepare **herbed butter** by combining softened butter with finely chopped herbs. Chives work well too. Roll herbed butter into a log shape using baking paper or freezer wrap. Chill in the refrigerator. Cut into rounds and freeze in zip-lock bags. Serve with fish, poultry and grilled meats. You can create many combinations of flavours including anchovy, capers, garlic, preserved lemon and sun-dried tomato.

capsicum (peppers)

To freeze **roasted red capsicum** (page 164) line a flat tray with a sheet of freezer wrap and place roasted capsicum on it in a single layer. Place another sheet of freezer wrap to cover. Freeze then remove from tray and divide into smaller portions. Freeze in an airtight container or zip-lock bag.

casserole & soup

Prepare double quantities of casseroles and soups and freeze in portions.

chicken & duck

Purchase whole chickens and ducks as you will have no wastage. Once you have jointed the bird (see below) use the carcasses for stock. You can freeze the carcasses and when you have two, you can make stock. See **chicken stock** (page 196). Prepare duck stock as you would chicken stock. I like to roast duck carcasses for both flavour and colour before making stock. The duck fat will render down after roasting so be sure to pour it off, strain and reserve. Store in an airtight container in the refrigerator. It will keep for months. It is wonderful to use when roasting potatoes. Use duck stock in soups with beans and lentils, in risotto and when braising meats.

Use poultry shears for jointing raw or roasted chicken, duck and quail.

To joint chicken and duck, cut down through the skin between the leg and the carcass, bend the leg back and it will pop free from the socket. Cut leg away from the backbone. Repeat the process with the other leg. You can serve this joint as a leg quarter or cut it in two so that you have a thigh and drumstick. If the breasts are to be cooked on the bone, use poultry shears to cut along the breastbone from the neck to the tail. Trim away unwanted sections of the backbone. To prepare boneless chicken breasts, use a sharp knife to separate the breast meat from the bone by following the contours of the breastbone. I like to have the option too of skin on or off the chicken breasts and thighs.

You can marinate chicken and duck portions before freezing. Defrost in the refrigerator when required.

chocolate — to melt

Melt chocolate in the microwave instead of messing around with a double boiler. For approximately 200 g (7 oz) couverture chocolate, place chocolate pieces in a microwave-safe bowl and microwave uncovered on medium for 1 minute. Stir and repeat at 30-second intervals until melted.

chopping boards

Use separate chopping boards for sweet and savoury foods. This avoids onion and garlic odours flavouring your sweet food recipes.

Place either a rubber mat, tea towel (dish towel) or dampened paper towel under your chopping board to prevent it from slipping when you chop.

chorizo sausage

Freeze **GF** chorizo sausage to have on hand as it is very versatile. Slice and pan-fry then add to tomato or capsicum sauce and serve with pasta. Use it in pilaff, risotto, soups and casseroles.

Add pan-fried slices of **GF** chorizo to frittata. A great combination is cooked sliced potato, spring onion, roasted capsicum, sliced pan-fried **GF** chorizo, parmesan cheese and parsley.

Add **GF** chorizo and prawns (shrimp) to pilaff.

cooling

To cool casseroles, soups and stock quickly, half-fill the kitchen or laundry sink with cold water, add ice cubes and/ or ice bricks too if you wish and place casserole, stockpot or saucepan in the water. The water should come about halfway up the side of the container. Refrigerate when cool. Fat will solidify on the surface. Remove and discard fat.

crepes

herbed crepes (page 207) freeze very well. Cook, cool and freeze crepes between sheets of freezer wrap. Omit herbs and use for dessert with sweet fillings. They are delicious layered with cooked apples and pears or lemon curd to create a 'cake' too.

eggplant (aubergine)

Brush slices of eggplant (aubergine) with garlic-flavoured olive oil and oven roast or grill until lightly browned and softened. Cool and then flat freeze on a tray. Use freezer wrap to separate the layers of eggplant. Once frozen, place in zip-lock bags or in airtight containers.

garlic

Microwave garlic on high for 15 seconds as this helps the skin to slip off easily. Use a microplane to grate garlic.

herbs & salad leaves

Grow your own herbs and a combination of salad leaves in a garden bed or in pots. Use a pair of scissors to cut stems of herbs. Use kitchen scissors rather than a knife to snip chives before adding to salads or other dishes. Oregano, rosemary, thyme, sage and bay leaves can be dried successfully.

Add herbs to casseroles and soups towards the end of cooking time as they lose flavour if added too early.

Basil does not like to be kept in the refrigerator. It will last out of the refrigerator for 5–7 days in a pot (jar) of water, covered loosely with plastic wrap.

To prevent basil from discolouring when making basil pesto, blanch the leaves ever so quickly, in and out of boiling water. Refresh immediately in cold water then gently dab with paper towel to remove excess water before making the pesto.

Basil pesto can be frozen. Cut a piece of freezer wrap measuring about 40 cm (16 inches) in length. Spread pesto on the freezer wrap into a flat rectangle approximately 30 x 15 cm (12 x 6 inches). Fold over excess freezer wrap to totally enclose the pesto. Flat freeze on a tray. When frozen, cut pesto in smaller portions, rewrap and place in zip lock bags or an airtight container. I prefer to use zip-lock bags, as containers tend to retain the smell of garlic.

Before spooning pesto over pasta, add a tablespoon or so of the hot water in which the pasta was cooked to the pesto. This will make the pesto more sauce-like.

kitchen timer
It is easy to become distracted once you have put something in the oven or on the stovetop to cook. It is useful to get into the habit of setting a timer so that you do not end up with a burnt offering.

lemons & limes
To extract more juice from lemons and limes, microwave on high for about 15 seconds.

Squeeze the juice from lemons and limes and freeze in ice-cube trays. When cubes are frozen, remove from trays and transfer to zip-lock bags. Freeze the shells of juiced lemons and limes. They will grate easily and can be used for flavouring sweet and savoury foods.

makrut (kaffir lime) leaves
Makrut (kaffir lime) leaves have a distinct, sweet fragrance. They are used in Asian cooking, in curries, soups and also shredded in salads. Keep a bag of lime leaves in the freezer. When cooking rice add several leaves to the water.

microplane
Use for grating parmesan cheese and garlic, zesting lemons, limes and oranges. Use a pastry brush to remove grated garlic and zest from the microplane.

microwave oven
I would not be without one! They are such a convenience for defrosting frozen food and for reheating food. Remember to allow 'standing time' as food will continue to cook. Always use microwave-safe containers. Some types of plastic are not suitable for microwave cooking. To avoid food from spitting, heat in covered containers or use plastic wrap that is microwave safe to cover. Pierce plastic wrap with holes if necessary.

muslin (cheesecloth)
Muslin (cheesecloth) is a fine cotton cloth used for straining stocks. If you are unable to purchase muslin, use kitchen super wipes.

oranges
Freeze whole and use for juice or follow tip as for lemons.

palm sugar (jaggery)
If your palm sugar (jaggery) hardens place it in the microwave and warm gently for a few seconds to soften. This makes grating the palm sugar easier.

passionfruit
Can be frozen whole or remove the pulp and freeze in ice-cube trays. When cubes are frozen remove from trays and transfer to zip-lock bags.

plating food
This means to place the food on a plate in such a way that it is appealing to the eye. As the saying goes 'you eat with your eyes'. Presentation really is important. The first thing we do is look at the food so colour combinations must be visually appealing. Choose different food textures, something crispy with something soft. Keep it simple. I do like to mould rice and rice noodles, soft vegetables and some salads as it gives the appearance of having gone to a little extra effort. Generally speaking, spoon sauces onto the plate and not over the food, but this really depends on the recipe. Wipe around the edges of the plate with a damp cloth so that it is clean and free of finger smudges. Most food looks good on white china although colour has its place. When using coloured china it should not clash with the food. Always warm plates and bowls when serving hot food.

potatoes
When cooking potatoes for a purée or potato mash, add one or two bay leaves (remember to remove bay leaves before mashing) or a grated garlic clove to the water to give added flavour to the potatoes.

Alternatively, fold in finely chopped spring onions (scallions), fresh herbs and/or parmesan cheese. Another healthy idea is to fold cooked lentils into mashed potato.

preserved lemons

I cannot live without them as my recipes attest. There is nothing mysterious about preserved lemons, yet they impart the most unique flavour to so many dishes. They are so simple to preserve yet expensive to buy. If you have a lemon tree preserve your own so that you can enjoy them year round. See **preserved lemons** recipe (page 202).

rice & rice noodles

Cook extra rice and freeze in portions. Add several makrut (kaffir lime) leaves to the water when cooking rice to serve with Asian food. They will give the rice a wonderful aromatic flavour.

Instead of spooning rice or noodles onto plates to serve, place cooked rice or noodles in ramekins or dariole moulds. Pat down, so the rice or noodles hold their shape and turn out onto plates.

sauces

Prepare double or triple quantities of **bolognese sauce** (page 105) and **easy tomato sauce** (page 200) and freeze in portions. You can have a meal ready in minutes with a few sauces on hand in the freezer.

skewers

Instead of using bamboo skewers, use firm rosemary stems stripped of all but a few leaves at the top or use lemongrass stems which are especially good for fish and prawns. Cut lemongrass stems in halves lengthways if thick.

spinach

Rinse and remove stems from spinach. Boil water and cook spinach in batches for several minutes. Remove spinach with tongs to a bowl of cold water and cool. Squeeze excess water from spinach. Separate leaves and place on a clean tea towel (dish towel). Place a second tea towel on top and roll up the spinach. Leave to rest for about 10 minutes.

Freeze spinach in layers using freezer wrap. This makes it easy to separate so you can use as much or as little as needed. Defrost spinach and toss in a pan with butter and/or oil and garlic to finish.

tomato paste (concentrated purée)

Freeze tomato paste in ice-cube trays and transfer to zip-lock bags when frozen.

washing up

Wash up as you cook so that you are not left with an enormous stack of pots and pans to do later. You want to be able to sit down with a cup of tea, coffee or a glass of wine and relax once you've prepared your meal, not be doing dishes!

wine

If you happen to have leftover wine, freeze it in ice-cube trays. Defrost cubes and use in cooking.

zip-lock bags

Storing food in zip-lock bags will keep food fresh for longer and save space in the refrigerator and freezer. Use for breadcrumbs, herbs, vegetables and cubed butter, ready for cooking.

Some zip-lock bags are suitable to use in the microwave. Always read labels first before using.

UTENSILS & OTHER COOKING AIDS

A well-equipped kitchen is vital for successful cooking. Good basic equipment is what you need. The simpler the tool the more you will use it. Here is a list of items I have in my kitchen:

baking paper, foil and freezer wrap
baking trays and roasting tins
casserole dishes with fitting lids
chopping boards for sweet and savoury food
citrus fruit zester
clear Pyrex measuring jug for liquids
colander
cooking twine
crepe pan (non-stick)
dariole moulds
digital scales
egg lifter
electric mixer
food processor
frying pans, non-stick and heavy-based
grater
julienne vegetable peeler
kitchen scissors
knives, the best you can afford
mandolin
measuring cups and spoons

metal cutters and pvc piping (the kind plumbers use)
    cut into varying diameters, for example, 6 x 5 cm
    (2 x 2 inches) deep, or 8 x 6 cm (3 x 2 inches) deep,
    used for moulding rice, salads, soft vegetables, etc.
microplane, for grating garlic and zesting citrus fruit
mixing bowls of varying sizes, stainless steel and
    microwave-safe
mortar and pestle
pastry brushes
piping (icing) bag and various nozzles
potato ricer for making creamy vegetable purées and mash
poultry shears
ruler or tape measure for measuring tins,
saucepans with fitting lids, heavy-based
scone cutters
shaker — used for dusting flour on work surface
spatulas
spoons — large metal and slotted, wooden
stick blender
timer
tins — various cake tins, spring-form cake tins,
    tart tins, muffin trays etc
tongs
whisks — large and small
wire racks
wire sieve

INDEX

Published in 2011 by Murdoch Books Pty Limited

Murdoch Books Australia
Pier 8/9
23 Hickson Road
Millers Point NSW 2000
Phone: +61 (0) 2 8220 2000
Fax: +61 (0) 2 8220 2558
www.murdochbooks.com.au

Murdoch Books UK Limited
Erico House, 6th Floor
93–99 Upper Richmond Road
Putney, London SW15 2TG
Phone: +44 (0) 20 8785 5995
Fax: +44 (0) 20 8785 5985
www.murdochbooks.co.uk

Publisher: Kylie Walker
Photographer: Jacqui Way
Stylist: Matt Page
Food Editor: Christine Osmond
Project Editor: Gabriella Sterio
Production: Renee Melbourne

National Library of Australia Cataloguing-in-Publication entry

Author: Moriarty, Pamela.
Title: Dinner secrets: gluten-free / Pamela Moriarty
ISBN: 978-1-74196-881-1 (pbk.)
Notes: Includes index.
Subjects: Gluten-free diet--Recipes.
Dewey Number: 641.56318

A catalogue record for this book is available from the British Library.

Printed by 1010 Printing International Ltd in 2011
PRINTED IN CHINA.

IMPORTANT: Those who might be at risk from the effects of salmonella poisoning (the elderly, pregnant women,
young children and those suffering from immune deficiency diseases) should consult their doctor with any
concerns about eating raw eggs.

OVEN GUIDE: You may find cooking times vary depending on the oven you are using. For fan-forced ovens, as a
general rule, set the oven temperature to 20°C (35°F) lower than indicated in the recipe.